... The code of Handsome Lake, the Seneca prophet

1735-1815 Handsome Lake

Nabu Public Domain Reprints:

You are holding a reproduction of an original work published before 1923 that is in the public domain in the United States of America, and possibly other countries. You may freely copy and distribute this work as no entity (individual or corporate) has a copyright on the body of the work. This book may contain prior copyright references, and library stamps (as most of these works were scanned from library copies). These have been scanned and retained as part of the historical artifact.

This book may have occasional imperfections such as missing or blurred pages, poor pictures, errant marks, etc. that were either part of the original artifact, or were introduced by the scanning process. We believe this work is culturally important, and despite the imperfections, have elected to bring it back into print as part of our continuing commitment to the preservation of printed works worldwide. We appreciate your understanding of the imperfections in the preservation process, and hope you enjoy this valuable book.

New York State Education Department
Science Division, September 11, 1912

Hon. Andrew S. Draper LL.D.
    Commissioner of Education

SIR: I transmit to you herewith and recommend for publication as a bulletin of the State Museum, a manuscript entitled *The Code of Handsome Lake, the Seneca Prophet*, prepared by Arthur C. Parker, Archeologist.

Very respectfully

JOHN M. CLARKE
    Director

STATE OF NEW YORK
EDUCATION DEPARTMENT
COMMISSIONER'S ROOM

Approved for publication this 16th day of September 1912

Commissioner of Education

The old log Long House on the Cattaraugus reservation formerly situated on the Buffalo "Plank road"

Photo 1900 by A. C. Parker

Education Department Bulletin

Published fortnightly by the University of the State of New York

Entered as second-class matter June 24, 1908, at the Post Office at Albany, N. Y., under the act of July 16, 1894

No. 530　　　　ALBANY, N. Y.　　　　NOVEMBER 1, 1912

New York State Museum

John M. Clarke, Director

Museum Bulletin 163

THE CODE OF HANDSOME LAKE, THE SENECA PROPHET

BY

ARTHUR C. PARKER

INTRODUCTION

HANDSOME LAKE'S ...

The Gai'wiio' is the record of the teachings of Handsome Lake, the Seneca prophet, and purports to be ... of the precepts that he taught during a term of ... years ... and his death in 1815. It is the basis of the so-called ... religion of the Six Nations and is preached or recited at all the council and winter festivals on the various Iroquois reservations in New York and Ontario that have adherents. These reservations are Onondaga, Tonawanda, Cattaraugus and Allegany in New York and Grand River and Muncytown in Canada.

There are six authorized "holders" of the Gai'wiio', among whom are John Gibson (Guniogwadon) and Edward Cornplanter (Soson'dowa), Senecas, and Frank Logan (Adodar'ho), Onondaga. Chief Cornplanter is by far the most conservative, though Chief Gibson seems to have the greater store of explanatory matter, often interpolating it during his recitations. Chief Logan is a devout adherent of his religion and watches the waning of his prophet's teachings with great sorrow. He is chief of the ...

The stated times for the proclaiming of the Gai′wiio′ are at the Six Nations' meeting in September and at the midwinter thanksgiving in the moon Nisko′wŭkni, between January 15th and February 15th. At such times the Oñgwe′′oñwekā or "faithful Indians" send for an expounder paying his traveling expenses and entertaining him during his stay. Usually reservations "exchange" preachers, Cornplanter going to Grand River or Onondaga and Chief Gibson to Cattaraugus or Allegany.

The time consumed in reciting the Gai′wiio′ is always three days. At noon each day the expositor stops, for the sun is in midheaven and ready to descend. All sacred things must be done sĕdē′tciā, early in the morning. Before sunrise each morning of the preaching the preacher stands at the fireplace in the long house and sings a song known as the Sun Song. This is an obedience to a command of the prophet who promised that it should insure good weather for the day. "The wind always dies down when I sing that song," affirms Chief Cornplanter.

During the recital of the Gai′wiio′ the preacher stands at the fireplace which serves as the altar. Sitting beside him is an assistant or some officer of the rites who holds a white wampum strand.[1] A select congregation sits on benches placed across the long house but the majority use the double row of seats around the walls. The women wear shawls over their heads and during affecting parts of the story hide their faces to conceal the tears. Some of the men, stirred to emotion, likewise are moved to tears but are unable to hide them. Such emotion once detected by the auditors sometimes becomes contagious and serves as the means of scores repledging their allegiance to the old religion. In 1909, for example, 136 Allegany Senecas promised Chief Cornplanter that they would stop drinking liquor and obey the commands of Handsome Lake. Visiting Canadian Oneida Indians at the Grand River ceremonies, as a result of such a "revival," petitioned for a visit of the Gai′wiio′ preachers several years ago, saying that a portion of the Oneida of the Thames wished to return to the "old way." This some of them have done but they complain of the persecution of their Christian tribesmen who threatened to burn their council house. In other places the case seems different and the "prophet's cause" is not espoused with much enthusiasm by the younger element to whom the white man's world and thought present a greater appeal.

[1] The original Handsome Lake belt is still displayed at the religious council at Tonawanda. (See plate 15.)

Those who live in communities in which the prophet's word is still strong are drawn to the ceremonies and to the recitals because it is a part of their social system.

Its great appeal to the older people is that it presents in their own language a system of moral precepts and exhortations that they can readily understand. The prophet, who is called "*our great teacher*" (sedwa'gowä'nĕ'), was a man of their own blood, and the ground that he traversed was their ancestral domain. Patriotism and religious emotion mingle, and, when the story of the "great wrongs" is remembered, spur on a ready acceptance. The fraudulent treaty of Buffalo of 1838, for example, caused many of the Buffalo Senecas to move to the Cattaraugus reservation. Here they settled at Ganŭn'dasĕ' or Newtown, then a desolate wilderness. Their bitter wrongs made them hate white men and to resist all missionary efforts. Today there is no mission chapel at Newtown. All attempts have failed.[1] Whether future ones will readily succeed is conjectural. The Indian there clings to his prophet and heeds the word of his teacher. At Cold Spring on the Allegany is another center of the "old time people." On the Tonawanda reservation this element is chiefly centered "down below" at the long house. On the Onondaga reservation the long house stands in the middle of the Onondaga village and the Ganuñg'sĭsnĕ'ha (long house people) are distributed all over the reservation but perhaps chiefly on Hemlock road. It is an odd sight, provoking strange thoughts, to stand at the tomb of the prophet near the council house and watch each day the hundreds of automobiles that fly by over the State road. The Tuscarora and St Regis Indians are all nominally Christians and they have no long houses.

The present form of the Gai'wiio' was determined by a council of its preachers some fifty years ago. They met at Cold Spring, the old home of Handsome Lake, and compared their versions. Several differences were found and each preacher thought his version the correct one. At length Chief John Jacket, a Cattaraugus Seneca, and a man well versed in the lore of his people, was chosen to settle forever the words and the form of the Gai'wiio'. This he did by writing it out in the Seneca language by the method taught by Rev. Asher Wright, the Presbyterian missionary. The preachers assembled again, this time, according to Cornplanter, at Cattaraugus where they memorized the parts in which they were faulty. The original text was written on letter paper and now is entirely de-

---
[1] See Caswell, Our Life Among the Iroquois. Boston, 1898.

stroyed. Chief Jacket gave it to Henry Stevens and Chief Stevens passed it on to Chief Cornplanter who after he had memorized the teachings became careless and lost the papers sheet by sheet. Fearing that the true form might become lost Chief Cornplanter in 1903 began to rewrite the Gai'wiio' in an old minute book of the Seneca Lacrosse Club. He had finished the historical introduction when the writer discovered what he had done. He was implored to finish it and give it to the State of New York for preservation. He was at first reluctant, fearing criticism, but after a council with the leading men he consented to do so. He became greatly interested in the progress of the translation and is eager for the time to arrive when all white men may have the privilege of reading the " wonderful message " of the great prophet.

The translation was made chiefly by William Bluesky, the native lay preacher of the Baptist church. It was a lesson in religious toleration to see the Christian preacher and the " Instructor of the Gai'wiio' " side by side working over the sections of the code, for beyond a few smiles at certain passages, in which Chief Cornplanter himself shared, Mr Bluesky never showed but that he reverenced every message and revelation of the four messengers.

HANDSOME LAKE

Handsome Lake, the Seneca prophet, was born in 1735 in the Seneca village of Conawagas (Gānoⁿ'wagĕs) on the Genesee river opposite the present town of Avon, Livingston county. He is described by Buffalo Tom Jemison as a middle-sized man, slim and unhealthy looking. He was a member of one of the noble (hoya'nĕ') families in which the title of Ganio'dai'io' or Ska'niadar'io' is vested, thus holding the most honored Seneca title. What his warrior name was is not known and neither is it known just when he received the name and title by which he later became known. It is known, however, that he belonged to the Turtle clan. Later he was "borrowed" by the Wolves and reared by them. His half brother was the celebrated Cornplanter.

The general story of his life may be gleaned from a perusal of his code, there being nothing of any consequence known of his life up to the time of his "vision." In 1794 his name appears on a treaty but whether he took active part in the debates that led up to it is not known. It is known from tradition and from his own story that he was a dissolute person and a miserable victim of the drink habit. The loss of the Genesee country caused him to go with his tribesmen to the Allegany river settlements. Here he became afflicted with a wasting disease that was aggravated by his continued use of the white man's fire water. For four years he lay a helpless invalid. His bare cabin scarcely afforded him shelter but later he was nursed by his married daughter who seems to have treated him with affection. His sickness afforded him much time for serious meditation and it is quite possible that some of his precepts are the result of this opportunity. His own condition could not fail to impress him with the folly of using alcoholic drink and the wild whoops of the drunken raftsmen continually reminded him of the "demon's" power over thought and action. In the foreword of his revelation he tells how he became as dead, and of the visitation of the "four beings" who revealed the will of the Creator.

After this first revelation he seemed to recover and immediately began to tell the story of his visions. His first efforts were to condemn the use of the "first word" or the white man's "onĕ'gă." He became a temperance reformer but his success came not from an appeal to reason but to religious instinct. The ravages of intemperance for a century had made serious inroads on the domestic and social life of his people. It had demoralized their national life and caused his brother chiefs to barter land for the means of a debauch. It threatened the extinction of his people. Such were the factors that induced the revelation.

He was a man past the prime of life, a man weakened by disease and drunkenness. Yet he assumed the rôle of teacher and prophet. In two years' time his efforts were conducive of so much reform that they attracted the attention of President Jefferson who caused Secretary of War Dearborn to write a letter commending the teachings of Handsome Lake. The Seneca construed this as a recognition of the prophet's right to teach and prophesy. The nature of the document is revealed in the following letter, a copy of which is in the possession of every religious chief of the Six Nations:

Brothers — The President is pleased with seeing you all in good health, after so long a journey, and he rejoices in his heart that one of your own people has been employed to make you sober, good and happy; and that he is so well disposed to give you good advice, and to set before you so good examples.

Brothers — If all the red people follow the advice of your friend and teacher, the Handsome Lake, and in future will be sober, honest, industrious and good, there can be no doubt but the Great Spirit will take care of you and make you happy.

This letter came as one of the results of Handsome Lake's visit in 1802, to Washington with a delegation of Seneca and Onondaga chiefs. The successful results of his two years' ministry became more fruitful as time went on. In 1809 a number of members of the Society of Friends visiting Onondaga left the following record of the effects of the prophet's teachings: " We were informed, not only by themselves, but by the interpreter, that they totally refrained from the use of ardent spirits for about nine years, and that none of the natives will touch it."

The success of Handsome Lake's teachings did much to crystallize the Iroquois as a distinct social group. The encroachments of civilization had demoralized the old order of things. The old beliefs, though still held, had no coherence. The ancient system had no longer definite organization and thus no specific hold.

The frauds which the Six Nations had suffered, the loss of land and of ancient seats had reduced them to poverty and disheartened them. The crushing blow of Sullivan's campaign was yet felt and the wounds then inflicted were fresh. The national order of the Confederacy was destroyed. Poverty, the sting of defeat, the loss of ancestral homes, the memory of broken promises and the hostility of the white settlers all conspired to bring despair. There is not much energy in a despairing nation who see themselves hopeless and alone, the greedy eyes of their conquerors fastened on the few acres that remain to them. It was little wonder that the Indian sought forgetfulness in the trader's rum.

As a victim of such conditions, Handsome Lake stalked from the gloom holding up as a beacon of hope his divine message, the Gai'wiio'. He became in spite of his detractors a commanding figure. He created a new system, a thing to think about, a thing to discuss, a thing to believe. His message, whether false or true, was a creation of their own and afforded a nucleus about which they could cluster themselves and fasten their hopes. A few great leaders such as Red Jacket denounced him as an imposter but this only afforded the necessary resistant element. The angels then conveniently revealed that Red Jacket was a schemer and a seller of land and an unhappy wretch doomed to carry burdens of soil through eternity as a punishment for perfidy. This was enough to create a prejudice among the Indians and one that lasts to this day among all classes of the reservation Iroquois. A few others endeavored to expose the prophet but this action only created a large faction that stood strongly for him.

Whatever may be the merits of the prophet's teachings, they created a revolution in Iroquois religious life. With the spread of his doctrines the older religious system was overturned until today it is to be doubted that a single adherent remains. Handsome Lake's followers were few at first. He was despised, ridiculed and subject to bodily insults. Certain failures to live up to a preconceived idea of what a prophet should be caused a continual persecution. Cornplanter, his half brother, continually harassed him, as may be seen in the relation. Some of his failures, real or fancied, caused calumny to be heaped upon him and they are current today among those inclined to scoff. It is said that he learned his ideas of morality from his nephew, Henry Obail (Abeal), who had been at school in Philadelphia. Henry, it is said, took him up in the mountains and explained the Christain Bible to him, thus giving him the idea of devising the Gai'wiio'. Other tales are that he failed to find the great serpent in the bed of the Allegany river though he pretended to locate it and charge it with having spread disease among the people, and that he erected an idol on an island in the river, a thing which from more authentic accounts he did not do.

Previous to his residence at Tonawanda he had lived ten years at Cornplanter's town and two years at Cold Spring. At the latter place he made so many enemies that he resolved to leave with his followers. This was in about 1812. With him went his chief followers and his family, among them his grandson Sos'hēowă who later became his successor.

Sos'hēowă was born in 1774 in the old town of Ganowa'gĕs, the home of both Cornplanter and Handsome Lake. Lewis H. Morgan, who knew him well, describes him as "an eminently pure and virtuous man . . . devoted . . . to the duties of his office, as the spiritual guide and teacher of the Iroquois."

Morgan gives a full account of the recitation of Sosehawa at the mourning council at Tonawanda in 1848[1] and credits the translation to Sosehawa's grandson, Ely S. Parker (Ha-sa-no-an-da).[2]

During the prophet's four years' stay at Tonawanda he became many times discouraged, "reluctant to tell," and though the people gradually became more friendly, he seemed loath at times to proclaim his revelations. Some Christian Indians have explained this as caused by an uneasy conscience that came with greater knowledge of the white man's religion but there is no evidence of this. During this stay he was invited to visit the Onondaga and this he did, though according to his visions it necessitated the singing of his "third song," which meant that he should die. In a vision which he related he saw the four messengers who said "They have stretched out their hands pleading for you to come and they are your own people at Onondaga" (section 122).

When the word was given, Handsome Lake with a few chosen followers started to walk to Onondaga. His prediction of his own death, however, caused many more to join the party when it became definitely known he had started. The first camping spot mentioned is at the old village, Ganoⁿ'wa'gĕs. Here upon retiring he commanded the company to assemble "early in the morning." At the morning gathering he announced a vision. It had been of a pathway covered with grass. At the next camp, at Gănundasa'ga, his vision was of a woman speaking. On the borders of Onondaga he discovered that he had lost a favorite knife and went back to find it. He was evidently much depressed and approached Onondaga with a reluctance that almost betokened fear. Upon his arrival he

---

[1] Morgan, League, p. 233, Rochester, 1851.
[2] Later known as Dioni'hogä'wĕ, *Door Keeper*, a sachem of the Seneca. Parker was Morgan's collaborator in writing the League of the Iroquois.

was unable to address the people because of his distress, so that it was said, "Our meeting is only a gathering about the fireplace." A game of lacrosse was played to cheer him but he could only respond to the honor by saying: "I will soon go to my new home. Soon will I step into the new world for there is a plain pathway before me leading there." He repaired to his cabin at the foot of the hill, in sight of the council house and there after a most distressing illness "commenced his walk" over the path that had appeared before him. He was buried under the council house with impressive ceremonies and his tomb may still be seen though the house has been removed. A granite monument, erected by the Six Nations, marks his resting place.

Handsome Lake lived to see his people divided into two factions, one that clung to the old order and one that followed him. After his death the older order gradually faded out of existence, either coming over to the New Religion or embracing Christianity. Thus by the time of the Civil War in 1861 there were only the two elements, the Christians and the followers of Handsome Lake. They stand so arrayed today but with the "new religionists" gradually diminishing in number. The force of Handsome Lake's teaching, however, is still felt and affects in some way all the New York reservations, except perhaps St Regis.

Handsome Lake as the founder of a religious system occupied such a position that his followers place implicit confidence in that system whatever his personal weaknesses and failures may have been.

"He made mistakes," said Chief Cornplanter, "many mistakes, so it is reported, but he was only a man and men are liable to commit errors. Whatever he did and said of himself is of no consequence. What he did and said by the direction of the four messengers is everything — it is our religion. Ganiodaiio was weak in many points and sometimes afraid to do as the messengers told him. He was almost an unwilling servant. He made no divine claims, he did not pose as infallible nor even truly virtuous. He merely proclaimed the Gai'wiio' and that is what we follow, not him. We do not worship him, we worship one great Creator. We honor and revere our prophet and leader, we revere the four messengers who watch over us — but the Creator alone do we worship." Such is the argument of his followers.

PRESENT EFFECTS OF HANDSOME LAKE'S TEACHING

There is no record of Handsome Lake's visiting Tuscarora, Oneida or St Regis. The result is that these reservations contain only Indians who are nominally Christian. The Oneida are virtually citizens, the Tuscarora as capable of being so as any community of whites, and the St Regis progressive enough not only to use all their own lands but to rent from the whites. Their "Indianess" is largely gone. They have no Indian customs though they are affected by Indian folk-thought and exist as Indian communities, governing themselves and receiving annuities. Their material culture is now largely that of the whites about them and they are Indians only because they dwell in an Indian reservation, possess Indian blood and speak an Iroquois dialect.

In contrast to these reservations where the Indian has become "whitemanized" stand out the reservations of the Seneca and Onondaga. On the latter the folk-ways and the "Indian way of thinking" struggle with the white man's civilization for supremacy. The Indian of the old way is arrayed against the Indian of the new way. The conservative Indian calls his Christian brother a traitor to his race, a man ashamed of his ancestors, a man who condones all the wrongs the white man has done his people, and a man who is at best an imitator and a poor one. On the other hand the Christain Indian calls his "feather wearing" (Adistowäe') brother, "a blind man in the wilderness," a nonprogressive, behind the times, a man hopelessly struggling against fate, a heathen and a pagan. Even so, the followers of Handsome Lake constitute an influential element and the other Indians are affected by their beliefs whether they are willing or not. As was remarked in the beginning, Handsome Lake crystallized as a social unit the people whom he taught and those who follow him today constitute a unit that holds itself at variance with the social and accepted economic systems of the white communities about them. They assert that they have a perfect right to use their own system. They argue that the white man's teachings are not consistent with his practice and thus only one of their schemes for deceiving them. They assert that they wish to remain Indians and have a right to be so and to believe their own prophet. They are largely instrumental in conserving the systems peculiarly Indian and though they are a minority they control a majority of the offices in the nations to which they belong. Among the Onondaga and Tonawanda Seneca they hold most of the offices. In connection with the Allegany and Cattaraugus Seneca I use the word control, advisedly, since there may be times when the majority of councilors may be of the Christian party. Even so, the "conservative" party controls enough to maintain the system that they deem right.

When their poverty is urged as an argument against their religion and social system they assert that the true follower of the prophet will be poor and suffer much in this world but that his condition in the " new world above the sky " will be in direct contrast. They therefore esteem poverty, lowly surroundings and sickness as a sure indication of a rich heavenly reward and point to the better material surroundings and wealth of their brethren of the white man's way as an evidence that the devil has bought them.

The writer of this sketch has no complaint against the simple folk who have long been his friends. For a greater portion of his lifetime he has mingled with them, lived in their homes and received many honors from them. He has attended their ceremonies, heard their instructors and learned much of the old-time lore. Never has he been more royally entertained than by them, never was hospitality so genuine, never was gratitude more earnest, never were friends more sincere. There is virtue in their hearts and a sincerity and frankness that is refreshing. If only there were no engulfing " new way " and no modern rush, no need for progress, there could scarcely be a better devised system than theirs. It was almost perfectly fitted for the conditions which it was designed to meet, but now the new way has surrounded them, everything which they have and use in the line of material things, save a few simple maize foods and their ceremonial paraphernalia, is the product of the white man's hand and brain. The social and economic and moral order all about them is the white man's, not theirs. How long can they oppose their way to the overwhelming forces of the modern world and exist? How long will they seek to meet these overwhelming forces with those their ancestors devised but devised not with a knowledge of what the future would require? My Indian friends will answer, " Of these things we know nothing; we know only that the Great Ruler will care for us as long as we are faithful." Asked about the clothes they wear, the houses they live in, the long house they worship in, they reply, "All these things may be made of the white man's material but they are outside things. Our religion is not one of paint or feathers; it is a thing of the heart." That is the answer; it is a thing of the heart — who can change it?

HOW THE WHITE RACE CAME TO AMERICA AND WHY THE GAIWIIO BECAME A NECESSITY

RELATED BY SO-SON-DO-WA

Now this happened a long time ago and across the great salt sea, odji″ke'dāgi'ga, that stretches east. There is, so it seems, a world there and soil like ours. There in the great queen's country where swarmed many people — so many that they crowded upon one another and had no place for hunting — there lived a great queen. Among her servants was a young preacher of the queen's religion, so it is said.

Now this happened. The great queen requested the preacher to clean some old volumes which she had concealed in a hidden chest. So he obeyed and when he had cleaned the last book, which was at the bottom of the chest, he opened it and looked about and listened, for truly he had no right to read the book and wanted no one to detect him. He read. It was a great book and told him many things which he never knew before. Therefore he was greatly worried. He read of a great man who had been a prophet and the son of the Great Ruler. He had been born on the earth and the white men to whom he preached killed him. Now moreover the prophet had promised to return and become the King. In three days he was to come and then in forty to start his kingdom. This did not happen as his followers had expected and so they despaired. Then said one chief follower, "Surely he will come again sometime, we must watch for him."

Then the young preacher became worried for he had discovered that his god was not on earth to see. He was angry moreover because his teachers had deceived him. So then he went to the chief of preachers and asked him how it was that he had deceived him. Then the chief preacher said, "Seek him out and you will find him for indeed we think he does live on earth." Even so, his heart was angry but he resolved to seek.

On the morning of the next day he looked out from the opening of his room and saw out in the river a beautiful island and he marveled that he had never seen it before. He continued to gaze and as he did he saw among the trees a castle of gold and he marveled that he had not seen the castle of gold before. Then he said, "So beautiful a castle on so beautiful an isle must indeed be the

Plate 2

So-son-do-wa or Edward Cornplanter, the Seneca teacher of Handsome Lake's Code

Plate 3

The Newtown Long House, Cattaraugus reservation. Chief Cornplanter lives near by.

Photo by George W. Kellogg
The Tonawanda Seneca Long House, near Akron, N. Y.

Plate 4

A typical family of the Seneca branch of the "vanishing race"

Photos by M. R. Harrington

A typical family at Newtown, Cattaraugus reservation. These people are all followers of Handsome Lake.

Plate 5

Onondaga Long House, Onondaga reservation. The Prophet's tomb is just below the spot marked +

The Long House at Pine Woods, Cattaraugus

Plate 6

Graves near the Onondaga Long House near Six Nations, P. O. Ontario. In the lower right corner the charred embers of the grave fire may be seen.

One end of the upper Cayuga Long House near Ohsweken, Ont. Note the Feast Lodge in the rear.

Plate 7

Seneca Long House on Six Nations reservation, Brant county, Ontario

Plate 8

Long House of the Canadian Onondaga, Grand River reservation. It is here that the feasts and thanksgivings for the products of the fields are held by the Canadian Onondaga.

Environs of the Cayuga Long House, Grand River, Ontario, Canada

Plate 9

Tomb of Handsome Lake, near Onondaga council house

abode of him whom I seek." Immediately he put on his clothes and went to the men who had taught him and they wondered and said, " Indeed it must be as you say." So then together they went to the river and when they came to the shore they saw that it was spanned by a bridge of shining gold. Then one of the great preachers fell down and read from his book a long prayer and arising he turned his back upon the island and fled for he was afraid to meet the lord. Then with the young man the other crossed the bridge and he knelt on the grass and he cried loud and groaned his prayer but when he arose to his feet he too fled and would not look again at the house — the castle of gold.

Then was the young man disgusted and boldly he strode toward the house to attend to the business which he had in mind. He did not cry or pray and neither did he fall to his knees for he was not afraid. He knocked at the door and a handsome smiling man welcomed him in and said, " Do not be afraid of me." Then the smiling man in the castle of gold said, " I have wanted a young man such as you for some time. You are wise and afraid of nobody. Those older men were fools and would not have listened to me (direct) though they might listen to some one whom I had instructed. Listen to me and most truly you shall be rich. Across the ocean that lies toward the sunset is another world and a great country and a people whom you have never seen. Those people are virtuous, they have no unnatural evil habits and they are honest. A great reward is yours if you will help me. Here are five things that men and women enjoy; take them to these people and make them as white men are. Then shall you be rich and powerful and you may become the chief of all great preachers here."

So then the young man took the bundle containing the *five things* and made the bargain. He left the island and looking back saw that the bridge had disappeared and before he had turned his head the castle had gone and then as he looked the island itself vanished.

Now then the young man wondered if indeed he had seen his lord for his mind had been so full of business that he had forgotten to ask. So he opened his bundle of five things and found a flask of rum, a pack of playing cards, a handful of coins, a violin and a decayed leg bone. Then he thought the things very strange and he wondered if indeed his lord would send such gifts to the people across the water of the salt lake; but he remembered his promise.

The young man looked about for a suitable man in whom to confide his secret and after some searching he found a man named Columbus and to him he confided the story. Then did Columbus secure some big canoes and raise up wings and he sailed away. He sailed many days and his warriors became angry and cried that the chief who led them was a deceiver. They planned to behead him but he heard of the plan and promised that on the next day he would discover the new country. The next morning came and then did Columbus discover America. Then the boats turned back and reported their find to the whole world. Then did great ships come, a good many. Then did they bring many bundles of the five things and spread the gifts to all the men of the great earth island.

Then did the invisible man of the river island laugh and then did he say, "These cards will make them gamble away their wealth and idle their time; this money will make them dishonest and covetous and they will forget their old laws; this fiddle will make them dance with their arms about their wives and bring about a time of tattling and idle gossip; this rum will turn their minds to foolishness and they will barter their country for baubles; then will this secret poison eat the life from their blood and crumble their bones." So said the invisible man and he was Hanĭsse'ono, the evil one.

Now all this was done and when afterward he saw the havoc and the misery his work had done he said, "I think I have made an enormous mistake for I did not dream that these people would suffer so." Then did even the devil himself lament that his evil had been so great.

So after the swarms of white men came and misery was thrust upon the Ongwe-oweh the Creator was sorry for his own people whom he had molded from the soil of the earth of this Great Island, and he spoke to his four messengers and many times they tried to tell right men the revelations of the Creator but none would listen. Then they found our head man sick. Then they heard him speak to the sun and to the moon and they saw his sickness. Then they knew that he suffered because of the cunning evils that Hanĭsse'ono had given the Ongwe-oweh. So then they knew that he was the one. He was the one who should hear and tell Gai'wiio'. But when Ganio'dai'io' spoke the evil being ceased his lament and sought to obstruct Gai'wiio', for he claimed to be master.

The Gai'wiio' came from Hodiänok'dooⁿ Hĕd'iohe', the Great Ruler, to the Hadiöyă'′geonoⁿ, the four messengers. From them it was transmitted to Ganio'dai'io', Handsome Lake who taught it to Skandyoⁿ′'gwadĭ (Owen Blacksnake) and to his own grandson, Sos'heowă (James Johnson). Blacksnake taught it to Henry Stevens (Ganishando), who taught it to Soson'dowa, Edward Cornplanter. " So I know that I have the true words and I preach them," adds Cornplanter.

NOW THIS IS GAIWIIO

The beginning was in Yai"kni [May], early in the moon, in the year 1800.

It commences now.

A TIME OF TROUBLE

The place is[1] Ohi'io' [on the Allegany river], in Diono'sade'gĭ [Cornplanter village].

Now it is the harvest time, so he[2] said.

Now a party of people move. They go down in canoes the Allegany river. They plan to hunt throughout the autumn and the winter seasons.

Now they land at Ganowoñ'goⁿ [Warren, Pa.] and set up camp.

The weather changes and they move again. They go farther down the river. The ice melts opening up the stream and so they go still farther down. They land at Diondēgă [Pittsburgh]. It is a little village of white people [literally, "our younger brethren"[3]]. Here they barter their skins, dried meat and fresh game for strong drink. They put a barrel of it in their canoes. Now all the canoes are lashed together like a raft.

Now all the men become filled with strong drink (gonigä'nongi). They yell and sing like demented people. Those who are in the middle canoes do this.[4]

Now they are homeward bound.

Now when they come to where they had left their wives and children these embark to return home. They go up Cornplanter creek, Awe'gäoⁿ.

Now that the party is home the men revel in strong drink and are very quarrelsome. Because of this the families become frightened and move away for safety. So from many places in the bushlands camp fires send up their smoke.

Now the drunken men run yelling through the village and there is no one there except the drunken men. Now they are beastlike

---

[1] The present tense is always used by Chief Cornplanter.
[2] The narrator, Handsome Lake.
[3] The Seneca term is Honio"oⁿ', meaning "our younger brother."
[4] The intoxicated men were put in the middle canoes to prevent their jumping into the water. The more sober men paddled from the outer canoes. This debauchery was common among the Six Nations at the beginning of the 19th century.

Plate 10

The "Time of Trouble" at Cornplanter's village. (See p. 20.) From a drawing by Jesse Cornplanter

and run about without clothing and all have weapons to injure those whom they meet.

Now there are no doors left in the houses for they have all been kicked off. So, also, there are no fires in the village and have not been for many days. Now the men full of strong drink have trodden in the fireplaces. They alone track there and there are no fires and their footprints are in all the fireplaces.

Now the dogs yelp and cry in all the houses for they are hungry. So this is what happens.[1]

THE SICK MAN

And now furthermore a man becomes sick. Some strong power holds him.

Now as he lies in sickness he meditates and longs that he might rise again and walk upon the earth. So he implores the Great Ruler to give him strength that he may walk upon this earth again. And then he thinks how evil and loathsome he is before the Great Ruler. He thinks how he has been evil ever since he had strength in this world and done evil ever since he had been able to work. But notwithstanding, he asks that he may again walk.

So now this is what he sang: O'gi'we,[2] Ye'ondä'thä,[3] and Gone'owo[n].[4] Now while he sings he has strong drink with him.

Now it comes to his mind that perchance evil has arisen because of strong drink and he resolves to use it nevermore. Now he continually thinks of this every day and every hour. Yea, he continually thinks of this. Then a time comes and he craves drink again for he thinks that he can not recover his strength without it.

Now two ways he thinks: what once he did and whether he will ever recover.

THE TWO WAYS HE THINKS

Now he thinks of the things he sees in the daylight.

The sunlight comes in and he sees it and he says, "The Creator made this sunshine." So he thinks. Now when he thinks of the sunshine and of the Creator who made it he feels a new hope within him and he feels that he may again be on his feet in this world.

Now he had previously given up hope of life but now he begs to see the light of another day. He thinks thus for night is coming.

---

[1] See plate 10.
[2] The Death chant.
[3] The Women's song.
[4] The Harvest song, see p. 95.

So now he makes an invocation that he may be able to endure the night.

Now he lives through the night and sees another day. So then he prays that he may see the night and it is so. Because of these things he now believes that the Great Ruler has heard him and he gives him thanks.

Now the sick man's bed is beside the fire. At night he looks up through the chimney hole and sees the stars and he thanks the Great Ruler that he can see them for he knows that he, the Creator, has made them.[1]

Now it comes to him that because of these new thoughts he may obtain help to arise from his bed and walk again in this world. Then again he despairs that he will ever see the new day because of his great weakness. Then again he has confidence that he will see the new day, and so he lives and sees it.

For everything he sees he is thankful. He thinks of the Creator and thanks him for the things he sees. Now he hears the birds singing and he thanks the Great Ruler for their music.

So then he thinks that a thankful heart will help him.

Now this man has been sick four years but he feels that he will now recover.

And the name of the sick man is Ganio'dai'io[2] a council chief [Hoya'ne].

THE STRANGE DEATH OF THE SICK MAN

Now at this time the daughter of the sick man and her husband are sitting outside the house in the shed and the sick man is within alone. The door is ajar. Now the daughter and her husband are cleaning beans for the planting. Suddenly they hear the sick man exclaim, "Niio'!"[3] Then they hear him rising in his bed and they think how he is but yellow skin and dried bones from four years of sickness in bed. Now they hear him walking over the floor toward the door. Then the daughter looks up and sees her father coming out of doors. He totters and she rises quickly to catch him but he falls dying. Now they lift him up and carry him back within the house and dress him for burial.

Now he is dead.

---

[1] See plate 11.
[2] Handsome Lake, one of the fifty hereditary sachems, or lords. Hoya'ne means, *perfect one* or *noble*, and is translated *lord* by the Canadian Six Nations. See Hale, Book of Rites, p. 31, footnote.
[3] Meaning, *So be it.*

THE PEOPLE GATHER ABOUT THE DEAD MAN

Then the daughter says to her husband, "Run quickly and notify his nephew, Tää′wŏnyäs,[1] that he who has lain so many years in bed has gone. Bid him come immediately."

So the husband runs to carry the message to Tää′wŏnyäs. And Tää′wŏnyäs says, "Truly so. Now hasten to Gaiänt′wakă,[2] the brother of the dead man and say that he who lay sick for so many years is dead. So now go and say this."

So the husband goes alone to where Gaiänt′wakă lives and when he has spoken the wife says, "Gaiänt′wakă is at the island planting." So he goes there and says, "Gaiänt′wakă your brother is dead. He who was sick for so many years is dead. Go at once to his bed."

Then Gaiänt′wakă answers, "Truly, but first I must finish covering this small patch of seed. Then when I hoe it over I will come."

Now he who notifies is Hätgwi′yot, the husband of the daughter of Ganio′dai′io′. So now he returns home.

Now everyone hearing of the death of the sick man goes to where he lies.

Now first comes Tää′wŏnyäs. He touches the dead man on every part of his body. Now he feels a warm spot on his chest and then Tää′wŏnyäs says, "Hold back your sadness, friends," for he had discovered the warm spot and because of this he tells the people that perhaps the dead man may revive. Now many people are weeping and the speaker sits down by his head.

Now after some time Gaiänt′wakă comes in and feels over the body of the dead and he too discovers the warm spot but says nothing but sits silently down at the feet of the dead man.

And for many hours no one speaks.

Now it is the early morning and the dew is drying. This is a time of trouble for he lies dead.

Now continually Tää′wŏnyäs feels over the body of the dead man. He notices that the warm spot is spreading. Now the time is noon and he feels the warm blood pulsing in his veins. Now his breath comes and now he opens his eyes.

---

[1] Meaning, Needle or Awl Breaker, one of the fifty sachems.
[2] Meaning, Planter, commonly called Cornplanter, the half brother of Handsome Lake. See p 136.

THE DEAD MAN REVIVES

Now Tää'wŏnyăs is speaking. "Are you well? What think you? (Isege^{n'} onĕnt'gayei' hĕnesni'goĕ')?"

Now the people notice that the man is moving his lips as if speaking but no words come. Now this is near the noon hour. Now all are silent while Tää'wŏnyăs asks again, "My uncle, are you feeling well? (onigĕnt'gaiye')."

Then comes the answer, "Yes I believe myself well." So these are the first words Ganio'dai'io' spoke ("Iwi" nai' o'nĕ't'gai'ye hĕ' nekni'goĕⁿ)."

Now then he speaks again saying, "Never have I seen such wondrous visions! Now at first I heard some one speaking. Some one spoke and said, 'Come out awhile' and said this three times. Now since I saw no one speaking I thought that in my sickness I myself was speaking but I thought again and found that it was not my voice. So I called out boldly, 'Niio'!' and arose and went out and there standing in the clear swept space I saw three men clothed in fine clean raiment. Their cheeks were painted red and it seemed that they had been painted the day before. Only a few feathers were in their bonnets. All three were alike and all seemed middle aged. Never before have I seen such handsome commanding men and they had in one hand bows and arrows as canes. Now in their other hands were huckleberry bushes and the berries were of every color.

"Then said the beings, addressing me, 'He who created the world at the beginning employed us to come to earth. Our visit now is not the only one we have made. He commanded us saying "Go once more down upon the earth and [this time] visit him who thinks of me. He is grateful for my creations, moreover he wishes to rise from sickness and walk [in health] upon the earth. Go you and help him to recover."' Then said the messengers, 'Take these berries and eat of every color. They will give you strength and your people with us will help you rise.' So I took and ate the berries. Then said the beings, 'On the morrow we will have it that a fire will be in the bushes and a medicine steeped to give you strength. We will appoint Odjis'kwăthĕⁿ¹ and Gayänt'gogwŭs,[2] a man and his wife, to make the medicine. Now they are the best of all the medicine people. Early in the morning we will see them and at that time you will have the medicine for your use, and before noon the unused medicine will be cast away because you will

---

[1] Dry Pudding. [2] Dipped Tobacco.

Plate 11

The sick man meditating. (See p. 21.)

From a drawing by Jesse Cornplanter

have recovered. Now moreover before noon many people will gather at the council house. These people will be your relatives and will see you. They will have gathered the early strawberries[1] and made a strawberry feast, and moreover will have strawberry wine sweetened with sugar. Then will all drink the juice of the berry and thank the Creator for your recovery and moreover they severally will call upon you by your name as a relative according as you are.'

"Now when the day came I went as appointed and all the people saw me coming and it was as predicted."

THE MESSAGE OF THE FOUR BEINGS

"Now the messengers spoke to me and said that they would now tell me how things ought to be upon the earth. They said: 'Do not allow any one to say that you have had great fortune in being able to rise again. The favor of the four beings is not alone for you and the Creator is willing to help all mankind.'

"Now on that same day the Great Feather[2] and the Harvest dances were to be celebrated and at this time the beings told me that my relatives would restore me. 'Your feelings and spirits are low,' they said, 'and must be aroused. Then will you obtain power to recover.' Verily the servants of the Creator (Hadio^{n}yä"geono^n) said this. Now moreover they commanded that henceforth dances of this same kind should be held and thanksgiving offered whenever the strawberries were ripe. Furthermore they said that the juice of the berry must be drunk by the children and the aged and all the people. Truly all must drink of the berry juice, for they said that the sweet water of the berries was a medicine and that the early strawberries were a great medicine. So they bade me tell this story to my people when I move upon the earth again. Now they said, 'We shall continually reveal things unto you. We, the servants of him who made us, say that as he employed us to come unto you to reveal his will, so you must carry it to your people. Now we are they whom he created when he made the world and our duty is to watch over and care for mankind. Now there are four of us but the fourth is not here present. When we called you by name and you heard, he returned to tell the news.

---

[1] The earliest of the wild strawberries are thought to be of great medicinal value and are eagerly eaten as soon as ripe. So sacred a plant is the strawberry that it is thought to grow along the "heaven road." A person recovering from a severe illness says, "I almost ate strawberries."

[2] The Osto'wä'gō'wä, the chief religious dance. See Morgan, p. 270.

This will bring joy into the heaven-world of our Creator. So it is that the fourth is not with us but you shall see him at another time and when that time is at hand you shall know. Now furthermore we must remind you of the evil things that you have done and you must repent of all things that you believe to have been evil. You think that you have done wrong because of O'gi'wē, Ye'ondă'thă and Gone'owo[1] and because you partook of strong drink. Verily you must do as you think for whatsoever you think is evil is evil.'"

GANIODAIIO COMMANDED TO PROCLAIM THE GAIWIIO

"'And now behold! Look through the valley between two hills. Look between the sunrise and the noon!'

"So I looked, and in the valley there was a deeper hollow from which smoke was arising and steam as if a hot place were beneath.

"Then spoke the messengers saying, 'What do you see?'

"I answered, 'I see a place in the valley from which smoke is arising and it is also steaming as a hot place were beneath.'

"Then said the beings, 'Truly you have spoken. It is the truth. In that place a man is buried. He lies between the two hills in the hollow in the valley and a great message is buried with him. Once we commanded that man to proclaim that message to the world but he refused to obey. So now he will never rise from that spot for he refused to obey. So now to you, therefore, we say, proclaim the message that we give you and tell it truly before all people.'

"'Now the first thing has been finished and it remains for us to uncover all wickedness before you.' So they said."

---

[1] See notes, p. 21.

THE GREAT MESSAGE

SECTION 1

"Now the beings spoke saying, 'We must now relate our message. We will uncover the evil upon the earth and show how men spoil the laws the Great Ruler has made and thereby made him angry.'

"'The Creator made man a living creature.'

"'Four words tell a great story of wrong and the Creator is sad because of the trouble they bring, so go and tell your people.'

"'The first word is One'ga'.[1] It seems that you never have known that this word stands for a great and monstrous evil and has reared a high mound of bones. Ga''nigoĕntdo'''tha, you lose your minds and one'ga' causes it all. Alas, many are fond of it and are too fond of it. So now all must now say, "I will use it nevermore. As long as I live, as long as the number of my days is I will never use it again. I now stop." So must all say when they hear this message.' Now the beings, the servants of the Great Ruler, the messengers of him who created us, said this. Furthermore they said that the Creator made one'ga' and gave it to our younger brethren, the white man, as a medicine but they use it for evil for they drink it for other purposes than medicine and drink instead of work and idlers drink one'ga'. No, the Creator did not make it for you."

So they said and he said. Eniä'iehŭk![2]

SECTION 2

"Now spoke the beings and said, 'We now speak of the second word. This makes the Creator angry. The word is Got'gon'.[3]

---

[1] Whiskey or Rum.

[2] Eniä'iehŭk meaning, *It was that way.*

[3] A certain number of the Seneca Iroquois still cling to the belief in witchcraft although they are loath to admit it to any one in whom they have not implicit confidence. While they assert that witchcraft was introduced among them by some Algonquin tribe which they had adopted, their early legends and traditions contain many allusions to witches and witchcraft. There are at least two distinct methods employed by witches to accomplish their ends. The first, it is claimed, is the older way and is the employment

Witches are people without their right minds. They make disease and spread sickness to make the living die. They cut short the numbered days, for the Creator has given each person a certain number of days in which to live in this world.

"'Now this must you do: When you have told this message and the witches hear it they will confess before all the people and will say, "I am doing this evil thing but now I cease it forever, as long as I live." Some witches are more evil and can not speak in public so these must come privately and confess to you, Handsome Lake, or a preacher of this Gai'wiio'. Now some are most evil and they must go far out upon an abandoned trail and there they must

---

of what is described by informants as analogous to "malific mental suggestion," either verbal or telepathic. Such witches were able to assume the form of ancient monsters, the nia"gwahē or *mammoth bear* being the favorite form. They had power of transforming people into beasts, of imprisoning them within trees without destroying the human nature or sensibilities of their victims. Many stories are related of how chivalrous young men fresh from the dream fast were able to release the unhappy prisoners from the spells that bound them.

The second and modern class of witches work their evil spells by introducing into the bodies of their victims by supernatural means a small needle-like splinter pointed on either end and having a central eye to which was tied the hair of the witch, a splinter of bone from the fibula of a deer, a worm or some like object. Instances where such things have been drawn from bewitched persons are commonly reported.

A witch can work fearlessly and successfully as long as she remains unknown to the victim and under some circumstances even when known. A "witched" person is often able to see as in a vision the witch wherever she goes and is likewise able to tell when she is about to approach the house. Witches fear the threat of an angry person to kill them. Such a threat if an earnest one is an effectual charm against further annoyance. To burn the object that a witch has introduced into one's body will torture the witch and kill her. Such objects are not often burned. If revenge is desired the victim, if sufficiently angry, can throw the object through space and injure the witch wherever he wishes. A person who successfully resists and destroys another witch's power may become a witch if so desired.

To torture a witch, force a confession and exact a promise of repentance, take a living bird, black in color (a hen is now usually employed) and carry it into the woods at midnight. Here build a fire and then split open the bird's body, extract its beating heart and hang it by its chords over a small fire to roast slowly. The witch will then exert every possible means to reach the spot and beg that the heart be taken from the fire before it is consumed. At such a time any promise may be exacted, for the witch is powerless. If the heart is consumed the witch will die of a "burnt heart." Witch poison may be extracted by putting fine sifted ashes on the afflicted part and staying

confess before the Creator alone. This course may be taken by witches of whom no one knows.

"'Now when they go they must say:

> "Our Creator, O listen to me!
> I am a miserable creature.
> I think that way
> So now I cease.
> Now this is appointed
> For all of my days,
> As long as I live here
> In this earth-world.
> I have spoken."

"'In this manner all must say and say truly, then the prayer will be sufficient.'"

So they said and he said. Eniaiehuk.

SECTION 3

"Now the beings spoke again saying, 'This is the third word. It is a sad one and the Creator is very sad because of this third word. It seems that you have never known that a great pile of human bodies lies dead because of this word, Ono'ityi'yende, the nigă'hos'sää', the secret poisons in little bundles named Gawĕn-

---

in bed until the poison comes out. The charm will then be found in the ashes. The spirits of great witches are able to return and possess another witch. A witch who has such a "friend" is especially favored, for in time of need the spirit-witch will direct her to money, goods or food. Witches do not always injure people who have offended them but more often their children or other near relatives. This is done that the person they desire to punish may see an innocent person suffer for their offense and so be tortured the more.

"Witch doctors" are of two classes: witches who are willing to pit their powers against other witches; and medicine men who have made a special study of the charms that will offset witch spells. This class may also be divided into two divisions, those who make a regular profession of dispelling witch influences, of discovering the cause of mysterious ailments, of extracting the object that causes the trouble and of identifying witches, and those who by reason of some special service they have rendered some spirit of nature have been rewarded with magical powers, great wisdom and immunity from malific influences. This class renders its services gratuitously. Small false faces worn on the person and frequent invocations of the Thunder spirit with liberal offerings of sacred tobacco are potent charms against witches. The False Face company has an annual ceremony in which witch spirits are expelled from the community. The I''dos company (q. v.) is said to be the survival of the older witch society introduced among the Seneca by the Nanticoke. Its members are reputed to possess magic powers.

nodŭs'hä (compelling charms[1]). Now the Creator who made us commands that they who do this evil, when they hear this message, must stop it immediately and do it nevermore while they live upon this earth-world. It matters not how much destruction they have wrought — let them repent and not fail for fear the Creator will not accept them as his own.'"

So they said and he said. Eniaiehuk.

SECTION 4

"'Now another word. It is sad. It is the fourth word. It is the way Yondwi'nias swa'yas.[2]

"'Now the Creator ordained that women should bear children.

"'Now a certain young married woman had children and suffered much. Now she is with-child again and her mother wishing to prevent further sufferings designs to administer a medicine to cut off the child and to prevent forever other children from coming.[3] So the mother makes the medicine and gives it. Now when she does this she forever cuts away her daughter's string of children. Now it is because of such things that the Creator is sad. He created life to live and he wishes such evils to cease. He wishes those who employ such medicines to cease such practices forevermore. Now they must stop when they hear this message. Go and tell your people.'"

So they said and he said. Eniaiehuk.

---

[1] Charms. Should a person die holding a secret, one may discover it by sleeping upon the ground with a handful of the grave dirt beneath his head. Then, *if all conditions are perfect*, the dead person will appear in three successive visions and reveal its mystery.

A young man, wishing to become a swift runner, may add to his powers by concealing in his belt a bone from the grave of some celebrated runner of the past. It is said that most famous runners of the League carried these charms.

A warrior who wishes to guard against sudden attack from behind may make an unfailing charm by cutting three slits in the back of his neck and rubbing into the wounds the oil extracted from the scalps of enemies. A peculiar soft white flesh will fill up the cuts and when completely healed will protrude. Should an enemy then approach these protruding scars will quiver and warn the warrior of danger.

The most effective charm for drawing riches is the tooth of a nia'gwahē.

[2] Meaning " she cuts it off by abortion."

[3] The Iroquois knew of such an herb. I find it mentioned by Dr Peter Wilson, the Cayuga, and it was pointed out to me at Onondaga in 1911. The Seneca and Onondaga belief is that every woman has a certain number of children predestined to them and that they are fastened on a stringlike runner like tubers, or like eggs within a bird.

SECTION 6

"'Now another message.

"'Go tell your people that the Great Ruler is sad because of what people do.

"'The Creator has made it so that the married should live together and that children should grow from them.

"'Now it often happens that it is only a little while when people are married that the husband speaks evil of his wife because he does not wish to care for her children. Now a man who does that stirs up trouble with his wife and soon deserts her and his children. Then he searches for another woman and when he has found her he marries her. Then when he finds her with child he goes away from her and leaves her alone. Again he looks for another woman and when he has lived with her for a time and sees her growing large, he deserts her, the third woman.

"'Now this is true. We, the messengers, saw him leave the two women and the Creator himself saw him desert the third and punished him. Now a sure torment in the after life is for him who leaves two women with child but the Creator alone knows what the punishment is for the man who leaves the third.'"

So they said and he said. Eniaiehuk.

SECTION 7

"'Now another message.

"'The Creator has ordered that man and wife should rear their children well, love them and keep them in health. This is the Creator's rule. We, the messengers, have seen both men and women desert each other when children come. The woman discovers that the man, her husband, loves his child and she is very jealous and spreads evil reports of him. She does this for an excuse before the world to leave him. Thus the messengers say that the Creator desires men and women to cease such mischief.'"

So they said and he said. Eniaiehuk.

SECTION 8

"'Now another message.

"'Tell your people that the Creator has ordered regular marriage customs. When the young people are old enough to marry, tell them so. When they marry they will live pleasantly. Now it may happen that the girl's mother discovers that she is very happy with her husband. Then she endeavors to make her daughter angry with her husband when he returns from a journey. But when the husband returns the young wife forgets the evil advice and greets him lovingly. Now the older woman, the mother, seeing this, speaks again hoping to stir up an ill feeling. Says the old woman, " My daughter, your spirits are dull, you are not bright. When I was young I was not so agreeable. I was harsh with my husband." Now the Creator is sad because of the tendency of old women to breed mischief. Such work must stop. Tell your people it must stop.' "

So they said and he said. Eniaiehuk.

SECTION 10

" ' Now another message to tell your people.

" ' The married often live well together for a while. Then a man becomes ugly in temper and abuses his wife. It seems to afford him pleasure. Now because of such things the Creator is very sad. So he bids us to tell you that such evils must stop. Neither man nor woman must strike each other.' So they said.

" Now furthermore they said, ' We will tell you what people must do. It is the way he calls best. Love one another and do not strive for another's undoing. Even as you desire good treatment, so render it. Treat your wife well and she will treat you well.' "

So they said and he said. Eniaiehuk.

SECTION 11

" ' Now another message to tell your people.

" ' This concerns short marriages.

" ' Now some live together peaceably and keep the family as should be. Then after a time the man resolves to go off on a hunting excursion in the woods for a certain number of days. So he goes, having agreed with his wife about it. All is well and he returns with a load of game. He feels well and thinks he is doing well in thus providing for his family. On his way homeward he meets some one who tells him that in his absence his wife has been living with another man. When he hears this report he feels sad and angry. He refuses to go to his home and turns from his path and goes to his relatives. Now whoever makes mischief of this kind does a great wrong before the Creator. So he bids his people to forever stop such evil practices.' "

So they said and he said. Eniaiehuk.

SECTION 12

"'Now another message.

"'Now this concerns both husband and wife. Now it may happen that a man and wife live together happily. At length the man thinks that he will go to another settlement to visit relatives there. His wife agrees and he goes. Now when he gets to the village he induces some agreeable woman to live with him saying he is single. Then after some time the man goes back to his own family. His wife treats him cordially as if no trouble had occurred. Now we, the messengers, say that the woman is good in the eyes of her Creator and has a place reserved for her in the heaven-world. Now the woman knew all that had been done in the other settlement but she thought it best to be peaceful and remain silent. And the Creator says that she is right and has her path toward the heaven-world, but he, the man, is on his way to the house of the Wicked One.'"

So they said and he said. Eniaiehuk.

SECTION 13

"'Now another message.

"'This concerns a certain thing that human creatures follow. It is concerning gakno'we'haat. Some men desire constant new experience, that is some men are always following yē'oⁿ'. Now it is a great evil for men to have such desires. This is a thing that the so sinful must confess. A man who desires to know gagwēgoⁿ yē'oⁿ'sho' will never be satisfied, for yē'oⁿ' will arise whom he can not know and he will fall flat. Now we, the messengers, say that all this is sinful and men must not follow such desires.'"

So they said and he said. Eniaiehuk.

SECTION 14

"'Now another message.

"'This is what your people do.

"'An old woman punished her children[1] unjustly. The Creator is sad because of such things and bids us tell you that such practices must cease.' So they said.

---

[1] Handsome Lake was ever the lover and champion of children. There are many instances in the Gaiwiio relating to the care and rearing of children. The mode of punishment here referred to was one of long usage. Sometimes the mother would fill her mouth with water and blow it into the face of the little offender, repeating until obedience was enforced. Punishment by violence as by whipping or striking was discountenanced. The mother

"'Now this is the way ordained by the Creator: Talk slowly and kindly to children and never punish them unjustly. When a child will not obey let the mother say, "Come to the water and I will immerse you." If after this warning the child is still obstinate she must take it to the water's edge and say, "Do you now obey?" and she must say so again and if at the third time there is no obedience then the child must be thrust in the water. But if the child cries for mercy it must have it and the woman must not throw it into the water. If she does she does evil.'"

So they said and he said. Eniaiehuk.

SECTION 15

"'Now another message of things not right.

"'Parents disregard the warnings of their children. When a child says, "Mother, I want you to stop wrongdoing," the child speaks straight words and the Creator says that the child speaks right and the mother must obey. Furthermore the Creator proclaims that such words from a child are wonderful and that the mother who disregards them takes the wicked part. The mother may reply, "Daughter, stop your noise. I know better than you. I am the older and you are but a child. Think not that you can influence me by your speaking." Now when you tell this message to your people say that it is wrong to speak to children in such words.'"

So they said and he said. Eniaiehuk.

SECTION 16

"'Now another message.

"'Tell your people that the Creator is sad because of what they are doing.

"'Some people live together well as man and wife and family, but the man of the family uses strong drink. Then when he comes home he lifts up his child to fondle it and he is drunk. Now we, the messengers of the Creator, say that this is not right for if a man filled with strong drink touches his child he burns its blood. Tell your people to heed this warning.'"

So they said and he said. Eniaiehuk.

---

who was intrusted with the care of children was accustomed to tell her children what was wrong and allow them by experience to know that her word was to be relied upon. A boy remained under the discipline of his mother until the age of sixteen when he was turned over to the training of his father. If the boy was unruly and without ambition the mother received the blame and was sometimes punished.

SECTION 17

"'Now another message.

"'Some people live together righteously as man and wife according as the Creator ordained, but they have no child. When this is so let this be the way: If the wife's sister has children, of these let the wife without issue take from one to three and rear them and thereby fulfil her duty to the Creator. Moreover when a woman takes children she must rear them well as if born of herself. We, the messengers, say that you must tell this to your people.'"

So they said and he said. Eniaiehuk.

SECTION 18

"'Now another message.

"'Tell your people that ofttimes when a woman hears that a child is born and goes to see it, she returns and says in many houses where she stops that its mother's husband is not its father. Now we say that it is exceedingly wrong to speak such evil of children. The Creator formed the children as they are; therefore, let the people stop their evil sayings.'"

So they said and he said. Eniaiehuk.

SECTION 19

"'Now another message.

"'Now the Creator of mankind ordained that people should live to an old age. He appointed that when a woman becomes old she should be without strength and unable to work.[1] Now the Creator says that it is a great wrong to be unkind to our grandmothers. The Creator forbids unkindness to the old. We, the messengers, say it. The Creator appointed this way: he designed that an old woman should be as a child again and when she becomes so the Creator wishes the grandchildren to help her, for only because she is, they are. Whosoever does right to the aged does right in the sight of the Creator.'"

So they said and he said. Eniaiehuk.

(So many words, Odi'waga″de, end of first day's preaching)

Recitation of the second day

SECTION 20

"'Now another message.

"'A way that was followed.

---

[1] The wisdom of the aged, especially upon ceremonial matters, was never questioned.

"'Sometimes a mother is ready to feed her family. When she is ready to bid them sit down, she glances out and sees some one coming and straightway hides the food. A woman visitor comes in. Now after some conversation the visitor says she is unwell and goes out. Then the family commences to eat. And the Creator says that who follow such tricks must repent as soon as they hear this message, for such practices are most wicked.'"

"Now the messengers said this."

"'Now the Creator made food for all creatures and it must be free for all. He ordained that people should live in communities. Now when visitors enter a lodge the woman must always say, "Sede'koni"," *come eat*. Now it is not right to refuse what is offered. The visitor must take two or three bites at least and say, "Niawĕⁿ'." Tell this to all your people.'"

So they said and he said. Eniaiehuk.

SECTION 21

"'Now another message.

"'Now this is right.

"'When a woman hears children playing near her lodge she must call them in and ask them to eat. The Creator says that this is right for some children are of poor parents and have little to eat. The Creator loves poor children and whosoever feeds the poor and unfortunate does right before him.'"

So they said and he said. Eniaiehuk.

SECTION 22

"'Now another message.

"'When a woman sees an unfortunate girl who has neither parents nor settled home and calls her in and helps her repair her clothing, cleanse herself and comb her hair, she does right and has favor in the sight of her Creator. He loves the poor and the woman does right before him. So we, the messengers, say that you must tell your people to continue to do this good thing.'"

So they said and he said. Eniaiehuk.

SECTION 23

"'Now another message.

"'The Creator is sad because of the sins of the beings that he created.

"'He ordained that mankind should live as social beings in communities.

"'Now it may happen that a woman sets out to destroy good feelings between neighbors by telling go'diodia'se (stories that augment by repetition). Now this woman goes to a house and says, "I love you and because I do I will tell you a secret. The woman in the next house speaks evil of you." Now heretofore the two women had been friends but upon hearing this story the woman becomes an enemy of her former friend. Then the evil story-teller goes to the woman whom she lied about and tells her the hard words that the other woman has spoken. Then is the liar happy having started a feud, and she hastens from house to house to tell of it. Now great troubles arise and soon a fight, and one woman causes it all. Therefore the Creator is very sad. Tell your people that such things must stop the moment this message is told.

"'Now the Creator has ordained another way. He has ordained that human creatures should be kind one to the other and help each other. When a woman visits another house she must help at the work in progress and talk pleasantly. If she relates jokes they must always be upon herself. If she speaks harshly of others the woman of the house must say, "I remember the desires of our Creator. I can not hear what you say. I can not take that evil story." So the trouble is ended there. Now the Creator says that the woman is true who refuses to hear evil reports. She cuts off the evil at its beginning and it does not go from her. So she has won favor before the Creator.'"

So they said and he said. Eniaiehuk.

SECTION 24

"'Now another message.

"'The Creator who made you is sad.

"'The Creator made every person with a different face.

"'Now a man talks saying that he is far more handsome than other men. He boasts that he is exceedingly handsome and grand. But the Creator says all this is very wrong. The vain must repent and never boast again.' So they said.

"'Now animals seem alike to you. A wild animal that you have once seen you can not easily say you have seen again. But people are different before you. Now when a man is handsome let him thank his Creator for his comliness.' So they said.

"'Now furthermore a man says "I am the strongest man of all. There is no one who can throw me to the ground." A man who talks thus is a boaster before the people. Now the Creator says that such boasting is evil. The Creator endowed the man with strength and therefore he should not boast but thank the giver who is the Creator. So tell your people these things.' So they said.

"' Now furthermore a man says, "I am the swiftest runner of the world. No one can outrun me." Now he regards himself as a mighty man and boasts before his people. Now the Creator says that such boasting is evil. The Creator endowed the man with his speed and he should offer thanks and not boast. So we, the messengers, say your people must cease their boasting.' "[1]

So they said and he said. Eniaiehuk.

SECTION 25

"' Now another message.

"' Three things that our younger brethren (the white people) do are right to follow.

"' Now, the first. The white man works on a tract of cultivated ground and harvests food for his family. So if he should die they still have the ground for help. If any of your people have cultivated ground let them not be proud on that account. If one is proud there is sin within him but if there be no pride there is no sin.

"' Now, the second thing. It is the way a white man builds a house. He builds one warm and fine appearing so if he dies the family has the house for help. Whoso among you does this does right, always providing there is no pride. If there is pride it is evil but if there is none, it is well.

"' Now the third. The white man keeps horses and cattle. Now there is no evil in this for they are a help to his family. So if he dies his family has the stock for help. Now all this is right if there is no pride. No evil will follow this practice if the animals are well fed, treated kindly and not overworked. Tell this to your people.' "

So they said and he said. Eniaiehuk.

SECTION 26

"' Now another message to tell your relatives.

"' This concerns education. It is concerning studying in English schools.

"' Now let the Council appoint twelve people to study, two from each nation of the six. So many white people are about you that you must study to know their ways.' "

So they said and he said. Eniaiehuk.

---

[1] A more complete catalog of the besetting sins of the Iroquois than set forth in the foregoing sections can not be found nor are they elsewhere more graphically described.

SECTION 27

"'Now another message to tell your people.

"'Now some men have much work and invite all their friends to come and aid them and they do so. Now this is a good plan and the Creator designed it. He ordained that men should help one another [1] (ādanidä'oshä').'"

So they said and he said. Eniaiehuk.

SECTION 28

"'Now another message of things not right.

"'People do wrong in the world and the Creator looks at all things.

"'A woman sees some green vegetables and they are not hers. She takes them wrongly. Now she is yeno^n'skwaswa'do^n', a thieving woman. Tell your people that petty thieving must cease.' So they said.

"'Now the Creator gave Diohe"ko^n [2] for a living. When a woman sees a new crop and wishes to eat of it in her own house, she must ask the owner for a portion and offer payment. Then may the owner use her judgment and accept recompense or give the request freely.'"[3]

So they said and he said. Eniaiehuk.

SECTION 29

"'Now another message for you to tell your people.

"'It is not right for you to have so many dances[4] and dance songs.

"'A man calls a dance in honor of some totem animal from which he desires favor or power. This is very wrong, for you do not know what injury it may work upon other people.

---

[1] The bee is a very popular institution among the Iroquois. See Museum Bulletin 144, p. 31.

[2] Meaning, "our life givers," the corn, beans and squashes. See Iroquois Uses of Maize, p. 36.

[3] One of the old methods of gardening was to clear a small patch in the woods by girdling the trees and planting in the mellow forest mold. The name and totem of the owner of the garden was painted on a post, signifying that the ground was private property. The clan totem gave permission to any hard-pressed clansman to take what he wished in emergency but only in such a case. These isolated gardens in the forests were objects of temptation sometimes, as the prophet intimates.

[4] The Seneca had thirty-three dances, ten of which were acquired from other tribes. See p. 81.

"'Tell your people that these things must cease. Tell them to repent and cease.'"

So they said and he said. Eniaiehuk.

"'Now this shall be the way: They who belong to these totem animal societies[1] must throw tobacco and disband.' So they said." "Now in those days when the head men heard this message they said at once, in anger, 'We disband,' and they said this without holding a ceremony as the messenger had directed."[2]

Eniaiehuk.

SECTION 30

"'Now another message to tell your people.

"'Four words the Creator has given for bringing happiness. They

---

[1] Animal Societies and Totems. The Seneca firmly believe that by using the proper formula the favor of various animals can be purchased. The animal petitioned it is believed will make the person successful in any pursuit in which itself is proficient. The charm-animal was sometimes revealed in a dream, sometimes by a diviner of mysteries and was often sought directly. A warrior wishing to become a successful fisherman, for instance, might do any one of three things. He might seek for a dream that would show him what animal would make him an expert fisher, he might consult a "clairvoyant" or he might go directly to a stream of water and selecting some animal petition its favor.

The patron of the fisheries was the otter and there is a special society of those who have the otter for a "friend." The Society of Otters preserves the rites of invocation and the method of propitiation and also the method of healing afflicted members.

Other animals which are thought to be "great medicine" are the eagle, the bear, the buffalo and the mythical *nia'gwahē* or mammoth bear that was alternately a man and a beast. To be ungrateful to these givers of luck is a sin that arouses the ire of the animal who will punish the offender by inflicting him with some strange sickness. The offense may be one of neglect or altogether unintentional and unknown. It is then the duty of the society to appease the offended animal by performing the rites on a grand scale that the individual has failed to do in the ordinary way. The ordinary individual ceremony consisted simply of going to the bank of some clear stream, in the case of the Otters for instance, and after smoking sacred tobacco, casting the pulverized tobacco into the water at intervals during a thanksgiving and praise chant. Then will the otters know that their human brothers are not ungrateful for the fortune they are receiving.

There were four societies, having as their genii the spirits of the bear, the birds (eagle), the buffalo and the otter, respectively, and taking their names from their guardian animal (Secret Medicine Societies of the Seneca, p. 113).

[2] This was done at the suggestion of Cornplanter who is accused of endeavoring to upset the plans and prophecies of Handsome Lake in many sly ways.

are amusements devised in the heaven world, the Osto′wägo′wa,[1] Gonē′owoⁿ′, Adoⁿ′wĕⁿ and Ganäwĕⁿ′gowa.'"

So they said and he said. Eniaiehuk.

SECTION 31

"'Now another message to tell your people.

"'The Creator has sanctioned four dances for producing a joyful spirit and he has placed them in the keeping of Honon′diont[2] who have authority over them. The Creator has ordered that on certain times and occasions there should be thanksgiving ceremonies. At such times all must thank the Creator that they live. After that, let the chiefs thank him for the ground and the things on the ground and then upward to the sky and the heaven-world where he is. Let the children and old folk come and give thanks. Let the old women who can scarcely walk come. They may lean against the middle benches and after listening to three or four songs must say, "I thank the Great Ruler that I have seen this day." Then will the Creator call them right before him.

"'It seems that you have never known that when Osto′wägo′wa was being celebrated that one of the four beings was in the midst of it, but it is so. Now when the time for dancing comes you must wash your faces and comb your hair, paint your face with red spots on either cheek, and with a thankful heart go to the ceremony. This preparation will be sufficient, therefore, do not let your style of dress hold you back.

"'You have not previously been aware that when a Godi′ont is appointed that you have not appointed her. No, for the Great Ruler has chosen her. A road leads from the feet of every godi′ont and hodi′ont toward heaven. Truly this is so only of they who do right before the Creator.'"

So they said and he said. Eniaiehuk.

SECTION 32

"'Now another message for your people.

"'He who created us appointed that there should be chiefs, (hodi′ion′), and that they should do good for the people.'"

So they said and he said. Eniaiehuk.

---

[1] The Great Feather dance, the Harvest dance, the Sacred Song and the Peach Stone game.

[2] *Honon′diont, overseers* or *keepers of ceremonies*, more often women than men. The word means *They are mountains.* (Hodi′ont is mas. sing.; **Godi′ont, fem. sing.**).

SECTION 33

"'So now another.

"'Tell your relations this. The Creator has sanctioned a feast to a medicine animal on a great day.'"

So they said and he said. Eniaiehuk.

SECTION 34

"'Now another message to tell your people.

"'Now the messengers said that this thing was beyond the control of Indians.

"'At some future day the wild animals will become extinct. Now when that day comes the people will raise cattle and swine for feast food at the thanksgivings.'"[1]

So they said and he said. Eniaiehuk.

SECTION 35

"'Now another message to tell your people.

"'You have been ignorant of this thing.

"'When the Honondi'ont go about to notify the community of a meeting for the celebration of Osto'wägo'wa, or for hearing the Great Ruler's message, the evil spirit at the same time appoints and sends another man, an invisible one, in his tracks saying, "Do not go. It is of no use, no benefit comes to you; rather do your own work at home and stay away." Now it is the messenger of the evil spirit that argues thus. Now know you that the evil spirit will hinder you in all good things but you can outwit him by doing the things that he does not wish you to do. Go then to the meetings. Then will the evil messenger follow you to the Long House and when from the outside you have heard the songs he will say that such is sufficient and that you may now return. Do not heed him but enter and take your seat. Then will he argue again saying that it is sufficient to listen and not take a part because you would not appear well in shabby clothing. Heed him not. Now this spirit speaks to your minds and his face is between you all.'"

So they said and he said. Eniaiehuk.

SECTION 36

"'Now another message to tell your people.

"'This will happen.

"'We have told you to watch.

---

[1] Pork is now the principal ceremonial food.

"'The Honon'diont will go out in fours for game for the feasts.

"'You may think that they are fulfilling their duty to Gai'wiio'.

"'The animals that fall must be thirty.

"'But this will happen when Gai'wiio' is new. The Honon'diont will kill twenty-nine and the twenty-ninth will be a cub bear. So there will not be thirty.

"'So this will be done when Gai'wiio' is new. It will be done at Adekwe'onge, the Green Corn thanksgiving ceremony.'"

So they said and he said. Eniaiehuk.

SECTION 37

"'Now another message to tell your people.

"'Now this is a thing to happen.

"'Hereafter we shall have a new species of deer.[1] The Creator will create somewhere a pair, male and female. The male deer will be spotted with white and the female striped with white over her back. This will be done and we say it.

"'Now moreover the messengers command that these animals shall never be killed.'"

So they said and he said. Eniaiehuk.

SECTION 38

"'Now another message for your people.

"'If all the world would repent the earth would become as new again. Because of sin the under-world[2] is crumbling with decay. The world is full of sin. Truly, this is so.'"

So they said and he said. Eniaiehuk.

---

[1] These deer are the sacred creations of the Great Ruler and as such no "pale invader" is permitted to see them, though a few of the faithful have at certain seasons seen them in the darkness fleeing from discovery. Cornplanter says these deer were killed by a jealous rival of the prophet while he yet lived, so defying the new command.

[2] The under-world was thought to be a dark region beneath the surface of the earth where were confined the creations of the evil-minded spirit. It was a vast cave full of winding chambers, dark turbid rivers, bottomless sloughs, hot springs and fetid odors, rapacious beasts, venomous serpents, poisonous insects and noxious weeds. The door of the under-world was guarded by the under-earth elves who had great difficulty in preventing the white buffaloes from escaping. Frequently they did and then began a great pursuit to kill or bring back the white buffaloes. At such a time the elves would tell the sun of the calamity and he would paint his face red as a sign to all the elves the world over that the chase was on. See Legend, Origin of Death Dance.

SECTION 39

"'Now another message to tell your people.

"'We, the messengers of the Creator, are of the opinion that the world will continue for three generations longer (or three hundred years).[1] Then will Gai'wiio' be fulfilled.'"

So they said and he said. Eniaiehuk.

SECTION 40

"'Now another message to tell your people.

"'The religious leaders and the chiefs must enforce obedience to the teachings of Gai'wiio'.'"

So they said and he said. Eniaiehuk.

SECTION 41

"'Now another message to tell your people.

"'This thing will happen when it is new.

"'Truly men will repent and reform but it will happen that three certain ones will neither confess nor reform. Nothing will induce them to confess.

"'There are grades of sin:[2] the sins of Hasan'owān'ĕ', the sins of Honon'diont and the sins of the ordinary people.

"'Now when you are preaching repentance, Gaiänt'wakă will say that these men when they pass from this world are most vile. He will say, "Let us cast them into the water for they are not worthy to be dressed for the grave. The Creator will not receive them." Now no one will object to what Gaiänt'wakă says.'"

Now this thing did happen as predicted and when the messenger arose the first thing that he did was to spread the news and give the command that it must not be done.

"Now they said, 'The Creator will not give up hope of them until they pass from the earth. It is only then that they can lose their souls if they have not repented. So the Creator always hopes for repentance.'"[3]

So they said and he said. Eniaiehuk.

SECTION 42

"'Now another message to tell your people.

---
[1] Handsome Lake taught that the world would end in the year 2100.
[2] The higher the position the greater the sin, is the prophet's rule.
[3] See p. 61, Idea of soul.

"'Chiefs and high officers have spoken derisively of each other and quarreled.[1] What they have done must not be done again.'"

So they said and he said. Eniaiehuk.

SECTION 43

"'Now another message to tell your people.

"'Good food is turned into evil drink. Now some have said that there is no harm in partaking of fermented liquids.

"'Then let this plan be followed: let men gather in two parties, one having a feast of food, apples and corn, and the other have cider and whiskey. Let the parties be equally divided and matched and let them commence their feasting at the same time. When the feast is finished you will see those who drank the fermented juices murder one of their own party but not so with those who ate food only.'"

So they said and he said. Eniaiehuk.

SECTION 44

"'Now another message for your people.

"'You have had the constant fear that the white race would exterminate you.[2] The Creator will care for his Oñgwë'oⁿwe (real people).'"

So they said and he said. Eniaiehuk.

SECTION 45

"'Now another message for your people.

"'Some of your relatives and descendants will say, "We lack an understanding of this religion," and this will be the cry of the

---

[1] Jealousy was the principal cause of the dissension that led to the decay of the League of the Iroquois.

[2] The Iroquois saw that the white race had encircled them and were drawing the lines ever tighter. They saw that they were in a position of great disadvantage, living as they did in the midst of a people against whom they had fought not only in their own wars but also as allies of the British. They saw how all other native tribes had been swept away with the advance of the invading race and thus no wonder they feared. Yet today (1912) they still exist unabsorbed and as a distinct people in the midst of the civilization of the Empire State under their own tribal laws and recognized nominally as nations. The story of how they have preserved themselves through three centuries of contact with an invading race that had little love for them and whose policy like their own in ancient times, is to absorb or exterminate, to accomplish a thing that no other aboriginal race has done, is well worth a place in history as one of its marvels. "Truly the Creator has cared for his red children!"

people. But even we, the servants of the Creator, do not understand all things. Now some when they are turned to the right way will say, " I will continue so for all of my days," but this will not be so for they surely will fall short in some things. This is why even we can not understand all things.' "

So they said. Eniaiehuk.

SECTION 46

" At the time of this prophecy I was in the Cold Spring village. It occurred at this time. The prophecy was then new.

" At that time a woman and her daughter administered a witch-powder[1] to a man and he lost his mind. He wandered off alone and died and thus a great crime was committed.

" Now at that time it was said among the head men, ' We will punish the women.' So it was the plan that each chief give the women one lash.

" Now I, Ganiodai'io' heard the resolution of the chiefs and was of the opinion that the women would easily survive such punishment, so, also, the chiefs believed it.

" Now all this happened when the head men sat in council, the four messengers being present.

" Now this thing must never happen again. Such councils never accomplish good. It is natural that foolish women should have done what these did.

" Now at the time of the lashing it was in my mind that they would surely live.

" So this must never happen again because the Creator has not privileged men to punish each other." Eniaiehuk. [See plate 12.]

SECTION 47

" So now another story.

" It happened that at a certain time a certain person did not honor Gai'wiio'. At a gathering where Gai'wiio' was being told this was done. It was at Cold Spring village.

"A man was standing in the doorway showing disrespect to the proceedings within. The prophet was speaking and as he said in closing ' It is finished,' the man in the doorway dainī''dädi. Now that was the last. The man did not go home to his dwelling and

---

[1] Witch-powders were used for various purposes but generally as poisons or love charms. Their use is condemned in section 3 and the punishment of those who use them in section 104.

Plate 12

The whipping of the witches. (See section 46 of the code, p. 46.)

From a drawing by Jesse Cornplanter

Plate 13

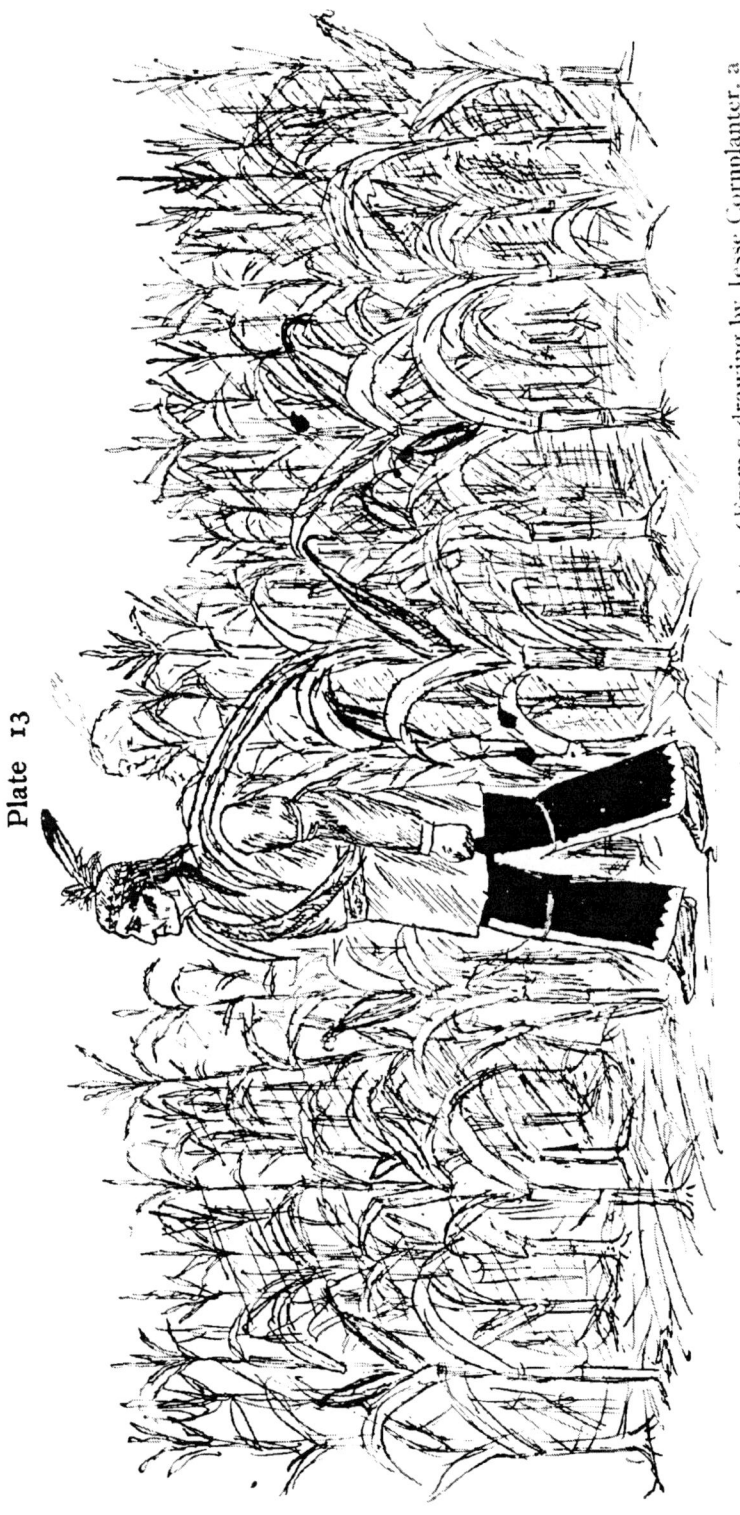

The Spirit of the Corn speaking to Handsome Lake, the Seneca prophet. (From a drawing by Jesse Cornplanter, a Seneca boy artist)

the next day it was rumored that he was missing. A search was made and on the other side of the Allegany in a swamp two days later the man was found. He was sitting above it. He had broken branches and arranged them in the form of a nest upon which he sat devouring snakes. He was not in his right mind. They took him from his nest (ho'noⁿ'gwae') and soon he died." Eniaiehuk.

SECTION 48

" Now another story.

1 " Now it was that when the people reviled me, the proclaimer of the prophecy, the impression came to me that it would be well to depart and go to Tonawanda. In that place I had relatives and friends and thought that my bones might find a resting place there. Thus I thought through the day.

" Then the messengers came to me and said ' We understand your thoughts. We will visit you more frequently and converse with you. Wherever you go take care not to be alone. Be cautious and move secretly.'

" Then the messengers told me that my life journey would be in three stages and when I entered the third I would enter into the eternity of the New World,[1] the land of our Creator. So they said." Eniaiehuk.

2 " The day was bright when I went into the planted field and alone I wandered in the planted field and it was the time of the second hoeing. Suddenly a damsel[2] appeared and threw her arms about my neck and as she clasped me she spoke saying, ' When you leave this earth for the new world above, it is our wish to follow you.' I looked for the damsel but saw only the long leaves of corn twining round my shoulders. And then I understood that it was the spirit of the corn who had spoken, she the sustainer of life. So I replied, ' O spirit of the corn, follow not me but abide still upon the earth and be strong and be faithful to your purpose. Ever endure and do not fail the children of women. It is not time for you to follow for Gai'wiio' is only in its beginning.' " Eniaiehuk.

SECTION 49

" ' Now another message to tell your people.

---

[1] The heaven described by Ganiodai'io' was called the New World because it had not been previously known. The generations before had not gone there, not having known the will of the Creator as revealed by the prophet.

[2] See plate 13, the Spirit of the Corn.

"'There is a dispute in the heaven-world between two parties. It is a controversy about you, the children of earth. Two great beings are disputing — one is the Great Ruler, the Creator, and the other is the evil-minded spirit.

"'You who are on earth do not know the things of heaven.

"'Now the evil one said, "I am the ruler of the earth because when I command I speak but once and man obeys."

"'Then answered the Great Ruler, "The earth is mine for I have created it and you have helped me in no part."

"'Now the evil one answered, "I do not acknowledge that you have created the earth and that I helped in no part, but I say that when I say to men, 'Obey me,' they straightway obey, but they do not hear your voice."

"'Then the Great Ruler replied, "Truly the children are my own for they have never done evil."

"'And the evil one answering said, "Nay, the children are mine for when I bid one saying, 'Pick up that stick and strike your fellow,' they obey me quickly. Aye, the children are mine."

"'Then was the Great Ruler very sad and he said, "Once more will I send my messengers and tell them my heart and they will tell my people and thus I will redeem my own."

"'Then the evil one replied, "Even so it will not be long before men transgress your commands. I can destroy it with a word for they will do my bidding. Verily I delight in the name Hanïssē'ono. It is very true that they who love my name, though they be on the other side of the earth, will find me at their backs the moment they pronounce my name."

"'Now at that time the Great Ruler spoke to the four messengers saying, "Go tell mankind that at present they must not call me Hawi'n'io‘, the Great Ruler, until a later time, for the Evil One calls himself the Ruler of Mankind. So now whosoever is turned into my way must say when he calls upon my name, Hodiänok'doon Hĕd'iohe', our Creator. So also whosoever speaks the name of the evil one must say, Segoewa'tha, The Tormentor. Then will the evil one know that you have discovered who he is, for it is he who will punish the wicked when they depart from this world.'"[1]

So they said and he said. Eniaiehuk.

---

[1] A typical example of Iroquois philosophy. The Iroquois were fond of devising stories of this character and many of them reveal the subtle reasoning powers of the Indian in a striking manner.

SECTION 50

" ' Now another message to tell your people.

1 " ' Now we are of the mind that the cold of winter will take life away. Many will be taken away because of the changing cold. Moreover some will freeze because they are filled with strong drink. Then again when the earth grows warm and the warm changes come, many will perish because of strong drink. Now the Creator never intended that variations of weather and season, warm and cold, should cause death.' "

2 " ' The Creator made the waters of the earth, the rivers and lakes. These too will cause death and some filled with strong drink will be swallowed up by the waters.' "

3 " 'And now more. The Creator made fire and this will also cause death and some filled with strong drink will be destroyed by the flames.' "

" ' Verily he has said and ordained that they who disobey Gai'wiio' should fall into hardships.' "

So they said and he said. Eniaiehuk.

SECTION 51

" ' Now another message to tell your people.

" ' The messengers have given the promise to the prophet that he will be able to judge diseases and prescribe remedies.'[1] So also he will be able to see far down into the earth as far as runs the elm's root. Then if any trouble comes and anyone asks the help of the prophet, he must give it freely, but they who ask must give an offering of tobacco. Now there will be some in your care who will be taken from your hands for other treatment. No wrong will be done and you must bear no ill will. It is said that the events of all our days are foreknown, so when the time comes for you to exercise your power we will tell you and then you may judge the earth and cure diseases.' "

So they said and he said. Eniaiehuk.

SECTION 52

" ' Now another message for your people.

" Now when my relatives heard all this they said, ' This man must be a clairvoyant (hĕnne'yoⁿ').'[2]

---

[1] See p. 113, medicine men.

[2] Diviners of mysteries have always been prominent characters among the Indians. Their office was to tell their clients the proper medicine society

"The news spread and Gaiänt'wakă came as a messenger.[1] Now he came to Ganiodai'io' and said, 'Why, having the assurance of powers, do you not commence now. Come prophesy!' Now he had tobacco for an offering. Then he said, 'My daughter is very sick.'

"Now the diviner of mysteries did not respond to his entreaty and so Gaiänt'wakă went out but soon came running back. This second time he had the same request and plead more earnestly, but without avail.

"Then it was said that he would not respond to the cry of a brother and had no hearing for the voice of a brother.

"Again Gaiänt'wakă returned and urged his brother.

"Now the people said, 'Have we not something to say to you as well as the messengers of the Creator?'

"Then he answered and said, 'Truly the people say that I will not reason. Verily I am true to my words. Now I can do nothing but try but I have not yet the permission of the messengers.'

"Now he went into a deep sleep and when he awoke he told his vision. Now he said that O'gi'we[2] should be sung for the sick woman.

"Now it is said that at that time the first song was in order but every part of the song was silent.

"Now a rumor spread that after all it was not wrong to continue the ceremonial dances once forbidden. So many were sick because they had not observed the commanded method of closing the societies."

This was so when Gai'wiio' was new. Eniaiehuk.

SECTION 53

"'Now another message.

"The four messengers arose from a sitting of the prophecy.

"Now he said that certain songs and parts of songs are not known and some societies are new and their powers untried. So

---

that would be most efficacious in curing the sick, to discover the whereabouts of lost children or articles, to discover what witch was working her spells, and to tell fortunes, as well as to interpret dreams.

[1] Cornplanter again endeavored to get his brother into disfavor with the four messengers by forcing him to exercise his powers prematurely. For this reason the followers of Handsome Lake to this day regard Cornplanter as a malicious character who ever tried to upset the Gai'wiio'.

[2] The death chant, a ceremony belonging to the O'gi'weono' or Society of Chanters. See the legend *Origin of the Death Dance*.

make a feast and throw tobacco instead of singing. But the chiefs said that that plan should be laid aside and notwithstanding, the songs should be sung as far as possible.

"Now the messengers said that they should secure provisions enough for the feast and be sure. Some have planned to have strong drink used at the feast but this must not be tolerated. Only food must be used."[1]

So they said and he said. Eniaiehuk.

SECTION 54

" Now I will relate another.

" There is a certain ceremony in the midwinter.[2] It is said that it is most important to uphold the customs of midwinter and that any one having a part should fulfil it. It is said that to fulfil the customs they must go about the neighborhood holding dances. It is said that the Creator has sanctioned certain dances for thanksgiving."

" Now the messengers said that Ganio'dai'io' must sing[3] early in the morning on three mornings and give the cheer-cries of the Gai'wiio'."

So they said and he said. Eniaiehuk.

SECTION 55

"' Now another message.

"' It is said that all your relatives and friends must be told.

"' It is said that when these rites are performed one person is to be selected to offer thanks[4] to the Creator. Now when thanks are rendered begin with the things upon the ground and thank upward to the things in the new world above. Afterward any one so inclined may arise and thank the Creator in the manner he thinks best.'"

So it is said. Eniaiehuk.

---

[1] It is related that at one period whiskey had so far debauched the Indians that their once sacred ceremonies, like those of the early Christians at Corinth, were made the excuses of the grossest licentiousness and drunken revelry. Whiskey had entirely supplanted the feast foods.

[2] See the Burning of the White Dog, p. 85.

[3] This song is still sung by the preacher of the Gai'wiio'. The preacher stands at the door of the Long House on three successive mornings of the new year's season and greets the sunrise with his song. It is said to be a charm against high winds and the faithful claim that Gao', the spirit of the wind, holds back his fury when the song floats over the settlement.

[4] See The Goneowo ceremony, p. 95.

SECTION 56

"' Now another message.

"This happened when Gai'wiio' was new. It was the time when he dwelt at Dionoⁿ'sodegĕ'.[1]

"A father and son appeared in Dionoⁿ'sodegĕ'. Now the name of the son was Gani'seoñ. They were on a hunting journey and came from Gadäges'käoⁿ[2] with a horse and cart. Now they tarried in Dionoⁿ'sodegĕ' for several nights before again taking up their journey.

"It was during the hunting season that the news spread that some one had returned from the hunting grounds without a companion. It was the young man who had returned. So they questioned him and asked where his father was. He answered, 'My father is lost. I went about searching for my father a number of days. I walked and searched and signalled with gun discharges hoping to find him. I could not find him and became weary waiting for his return.' So he said."

"Now Gaiänt'wakă when he heard this said, ' It is apparent to me that the young man has spoken the untruth.' So then they all went to the diviner of mysteries and Gaiänt'wakă spoke to him saying, 'It is my opinion that the boy has murdered his own father.' And the prophet answering said, ' They have not yet given me the power to see things but this will I do. Bring a bullet, a knife, and a hatchet that the boy may look upon these things when I speak and perhaps the truth will come (*see* plate 14). One of these things will move though not touched and he shall be the witness.' So the head men did as bidden and placed the objects as directed. In the middle of the floor they spread a blanket and put the articles upon it. Then they gathered around it and watched, and as they watched he spoke and the bullet moved. Thus it happened. Then spoke Ganio'dai'io', ' This brings the confirmation of the rumor. Truly the youth has murdered his father, and furthermore I say that the crime was committed between Gānos'[3] and Hanĕnk'gaek.[4] On the south side of a mountain, where half way up an elm is broken, leaning over on the downhill side to the west lies the body buried in the leaves of the top branches. He, the father, is buried in the leaves.' So he said when he spoke. The

---

[1] Cornplanter village.
[2] Cattaraugus village, the principal town of the Cattaraugus region.
[3] Franklin, Pa.
[4] Oil City, Pa.

Plate 14

The discovery of the murderer, section 56. (See p. 52.)

From a drawing by Jesse Cornplanter

chiefs and head-men appointed a delegation to see if all he had said were true. So they went as they had been told and found the body of the father and brought it back with them." Eniaiehuk.

SECTION 57

"'Now another message to tell your people.

"'You may ask three questions concerning three privileges when you go among your relatives at the ceremony of Nĭsko′wŭknĭ[1] and ask what one is fitted for them.

"'Who among you likes best to call upon the afflicted? Who among you loves to commune alone in the forests? Who among you is most anxious concerning religious conditions?'"

So they asked him. Eniaiehuk.

SECTION 58

"'Now another message.

"'Now this matter will devolve upon you.

"'The people will assemble in council and ask, "Who among us is able to say, 'I compel you to assemble?'"

"'Now when the question is set forth each person must make reply. The chiefs must demand it.'

"Now it happened that he fulfilled the requirements and all the people assembled and with one accord acclaimed that Ganio'dai'io' should lead them and that they should never murmur.

"Now that the people had done, he was patient to learn the result.

"The council adjourned and the messengers came and questioned him saying, 'How did you understand your people?'

"He answered, 'The majority consented that I should lead them.'[2]

"Then the messengers replied, 'Truly the greater number will follow you.'"

So they said and he said. Eniaiehuk.

SECTION 59

"'Now another message.

"'It is this: We, the messengers of our Creator, see strong drink used during the season when corn is planted. Now let those

---

[1] February, the moon of the midwinter, the time of thanksgiving.

[2] Because the people of this council elected that Handsome Lake should have authority over them he is ever after called Sĕdwāgo′wănĕ, or chief leader, or our great teacher.

who use this evil drink know that it consumes the elements of life They must repent.'"

So they said and he said. Eniaiehuk.

SECTION 60

"'Now another message.

"'It is a custom for thanksgiving to be made over the hills of planted corn.[1] Let the head one of the family make an invocation over the planted hills that the corn may continue to support life. Now this will be a right thing and whosoever asks the help of the Creator will receive it.'"

So they said and he said. Eniaiehuk.

SECTION 61.

"'So now another.

"'Now it is understood that Dio'he"'ko^n (the corn, bean and squash spirits), have a secret medicine, o'sagan'dă' and o'sdĭs'dani. So soak your seed corn in these two medicines before you plant your fields. The medicines grow on the flat lands near streams.'"

So they said and he said. Eniaiehuk.

SECTION 62

"'Now another message.

"'Now there are some who have boasted that they could drink all the strong drink in the world. Now we, the messengers, say that they who thus idly boast will never live to accomplish what they boast. White men will ever distil the evil liquor.'"[2]

So they said and he said. Eniaiehuk.

SECTION 63

"'Now another message.

"'Tell your friends and relatives that there will be two divisions

---

[1] The ceremony of invoking the Creator over the hills of corn was an old one and like many other old customs was indorsed by the prophet. This custom is still continued among some of the Iroquois. "When the leaf of the dogwood is the size of a squirrel's ear, the planting season has come. Before the dawn of the first day of the planting a virgin girl is sent to the fields where she scatters a few grains of corn to the earth as she invokes the assistance of the spirit of the corn for the harvest."

[2] This section with others of similar import brings out the prophet's intense dislike of idle boasting.

of mind[1] among the chiefs and head-men and among the people. Nevermore will your race be united.'"

So they said and he said. Eniaiehuk.

SECTION 64

"'Now another message.

"Now the messengers commanded him to give attention and he did. Then he saw a great assembly and the assembly was singing:

> 'The whole earth is here assembled,
> The whole world may come to us.
> We are ready.'

"Then said the messengers, 'What did you see when you gave attention?'

"He answered, 'I saw a great gathering of beings and the gathering was singing and the words of the song were:

> 'The whole earth is here assembled,
> The whole world may come to us.
> We are ready.'

"Then said the messengers, 'It is very true. The beings that you saw resemble human creatures. It is true that they are singing. Now the assembly is a gathered host of medicines for healing. Now let this be your ceremony when you wish to employ the medicine in a plant: First offer tobacco. Then tell the plant in gentle words what you desire of it and pluck it from the roots. It is said in the upper world that it is not right to take a plant for medicine without first talking to it. Let not one ever be taken without first speaking.'"[2]

So they said and he said. Eniaiehuk.

---

[1] This seemingly obscure section is cleared of its mystery when the preacher explains that the divisions of mind refer to the Gaiwios'tŭk or Christian and Oñgwe'oⁿwekā' or Indian parties. "Dewadia'ke' gani'goi', broken in twain, the unity of purpose," is Chief Cornplanter's term.

[2] The ceremony of gathering herbs. When a Seneca wishes to gather medicinal herbs, he goes into the woods where they grow and builds a small fire. When there is a quantity of glowing embers he stands before it and as he speaks at intervals casts a pinch of tobacco on the coals. He speaks to the spirits of the medicines telling them that he desires their healing virtues to cure his people of their afflictions.

"You have said that you are ready to heal the earth," chants the gatherer of herbs, "so now I claim you for my medicine. Give me of your healing virtues to purge and cleanse and cure. I will not destroy you but plant your seed that you may come again and yield fourfold more. Spirits of the herbs, I do not take your lives without purpose but to make you the agent of heal-

SECTION 65

"'Now another message.

"'It has been a custom when a person knows of a healing herb to ask payment for giving it to a patient. Now we say that this is not right. It is not right to demand compensation for treating the sick. If such is done it adds greater afflictions to the sick one. The Creator has given different people knowledge of different things and it is the Creator's desire that men should employ their knowledge to help one another, especially those who are afflicted. Now moreover the person helped out ought only to give tobacco for an offering.'"

So they said and he said. Eniaiehuk.

SECTION 66

"'Now another message.

"'Now it is said that your fathers of old never reached the true lands of our Creator nor did they ever enter the house of the tormentor, Ganos'ge'.[1] It is said that in some matters they did the will of the Creator and that in others they did not. They did both good and bad and none was either good or bad. They are therefore in a place separate and unknown to us, we think, enjoying themselves.'"

So they said and he said. Eniaiehuk.

SECTION 67

"'Now another message.

"'Now it is said that your people must change certain customs. It has been the custom to mourn at each recurring anniversary of the death of a friend or relative.[2] It is said that while you are

---

ing, for we are very sick. You have said that all the world might come to you, so I have come. I give you thanks for your benefits and thank the Creator for your gift."

When the last puff of tobacco smoke had arisen the gatherer of herbs begins his work. He digs the plant from the roots and breaking off the seed stalks drops the pods into the hole and gently covers them over with fertile leaf mold.

"The plant will come again," he says, "and I have not destroyed life but helped increase it. So the plant is willing to lend me of its virtue." Gahadondeh, (Woodland Border). Seneca.

[1] The evil spirit has no domain except his house. A land in which the condemned spirit might roam would not be so terrible but eternal confinement within a house was considered a horrible fate by the liberty-loving Iroquois.

[2] See Funeral and Mourning Customs, p. 107.

upon the earth you do not realize the harm that this works upon the departed.

"'Now moreover it is said that when an infant is born upon the earth with which the parents are dissatisfied, it knows and says, "I will return to my home above the earth."'"

"Now it is said that our grief adds to the sorrows of the dead. It is said that it is not possible to grieve always. Ten days shall be the time for mourning and when our friends depart we must lay grief aside. When you, the beings of earth, lose one of your number you must bury your grief in their grave. Some will die today and some tomorrow for the number of our days is known in the sky-world. So hereafter do not grieve. Now it is said that when the ten days have elapsed to prepare a feast and the soul of the dead will return and partake of it with you. It is said moreover that you can journey with the dead only as far as the grave. It is said that when you follow a body to the grave you must have prepared for that journey as if to travel afar. Put on your finest clothing for every human creature is on its journey graveward. It is said that the bodies of the dead have intelligence and know what transpires about them.[1] It is true.'"

So they said and he said. Eniaiehuk.

SECTION 68

"Now it is said that when Ganio'dai'io' was at Tonawanda spreading Gai'wiio' it happened that a certain man named Segwai''do"gwi said, 'I will also send a message to the four messengers and ask whether I am right in my belief in repentance and right doing.' So he sent his message upward in tobacco smoke."

Now when the messengers arose from a council with Ganio'dai'io' he reported what they had told him. "It is a hard matter for he, the questioner, is two-minded." So he said.

Then Segwai''do"gwi said, "Now this will I do: I will give a string of wampum, ot'go'ä, to the chiefs for a proof of my repentance, for though I have been thinking, yet I can not discover that I am two-minded."

Now when Gai'wiiostŭk (the Christian religion) came this man was the first to accept its teaching. When the chiefs heard of it they went to him and offered to return his wampum.

Then said the man, "I will not turn back because it is for the good of all that I have this religion."

---
[1] See, The death feast, p. 110.

Now all the chiefs and head-men could not persuade him to return to the right way.

So it is said. Eniaiehuk.

SECTION 69

" Now another message.

" Now it is said that you must relate what the messengers say about the coming end of the earth. Relate how all those who refuse to believe in Gai'wiio' will suffer hardships.[1] Now when the earth is about to end the chiefs and head-men will disagree and that will be a sign. So also, the Honon'doint will disagree. Then will the relations know the truth."

So they said and he said. Eniaiehuk.

SECTION 70

" Now another message.

" Now we say that you must tell your friends and relatives that there will be a time when all the earth will withhold its sustaining foods. Then will come the end of the world and those who refuse to believe in Gai'wiio' will suffer great hardships."

So they said and he said. Eniaiehuk.

SECTION 71

" Now another message.

" Now we think that a time will come when a great plague will kill many people and no one will know its cause. Then will you know that the end is near and those who do not believe will suffer great hardships."

So they said and he said. Eniaiehuk.

SECTION 72

" Now another message.

" Now we think that a time will come when a woman will be seen performing her witch spells in the daylight. Then will you know that the end is near. She will run through the neighborhood boasting how many she has slain by her sorcery. Then will you see how she who refused to believe in Gai'wiio' will suffer punishment."

So they said and he said. Eniaiehuk.

SECTION 73

" Now another message.

" In that time you will hear many rumors of men who say, ' I have spoken with the Creator.' So also will you see many wonders

---
[1] See Introduction, p. 26.

but they will not endure for they will be the work of the evil spirit.

"Verily we say that there will be none other than you who will receive a message from the Creator through us. This truth will be proclaimed when the end comes."

So they said and he said. Eniaiehuk.

SECTION 74

"Now another message.

"In that time every poisonous creature will appear. These creatures the Creator has imprisoned in the underworld and they are the creations of the evil-minded spirit. Now it is our opinion that when they are released many people will be captured and poisoned by them. Men will see these hardships when they fail to believe in Gai'wiio'."

So they said and he said. Eniaiehuk.

SECTION 75

"Now another message.

"Now there will be some who will enter into a sleep. When they lie down they will be in health and as they sleep the Creator will withdraw their lives for they are true. To the faithful this will happen."[1]

So they said and he said. Eniaiehuk.

SECTION 76

"Now another message.

"Now we think that the Creator will stop the earth and heavens. All the powers of nature will he suspend. Now they will see this who refuse to believe in Gai'wiio'."

So they said and he said. Eniaiehuk.

SECTION 77

"Now another message.

"Now we think that when the end comes the earth will be destroyed by fire and not one upon it will escape for all the earth will be enveloped in flames and all those who refuse to believe in Gai'wiio' will be in it."

So they said and he said. Eniaiehuk.

---

[1] Because Handsome Lake did not die in this manner some of his half believing followers at Onondaga repudiated his teaching.

Recitation of the third day

NOW AT TONAWANDA

SECTION 78

"Now another message. Tell it to those at Tonawanda.

"Now they said to him, ' Watch a certain place.' So he did and he saw a certain person holding meat in his hands. The man was rejoicing and was well clothed and fed and his name was Tă'dondä'ieha', and he recognized him."

"Then said they to him, ' How is it? '"

"He answered, ' I recognized Tă'dondä'ieha' and he held meat in his hands.' So answered he who talked religiously."

"Then the messengers answered, ' Truly you saw a man with meat enjoying himself. He was joyous because he was a prosperous and successful hunter and gave game as presents to his neighbors. So his neighbors were grateful and thanked him. Now the man you saw has departed from the earth. In his earth-life he cleansed himself each day, visited and enjoyed himself in his best clothing. He was ever good to his fellow-beings and so he is blessed and will receive the reward reserved for him by his Creator."

So they said and he said. Eniaiehuk.

SECTION 79

"Now another message.

"This will happen.

"You will sing three times and the third time you sing you will step into oyă'dedion'diade', the other world.[1] That you go there will be the earnest wish of all who have heard your message."

So they said and he said. Eniaiehuk.

SECTION 80

"Now another message.

"Every person has a song to sing when the time comes to leave the earth. When a person is departing he must sing that song

---

[1] It was customary for the friends and relatives to address the body of the dead and give expression to one's desires, etc. The soul when it reached the heaven-world would then tell the Great Ruler who would attend to the wishes expressed.

Plate 15

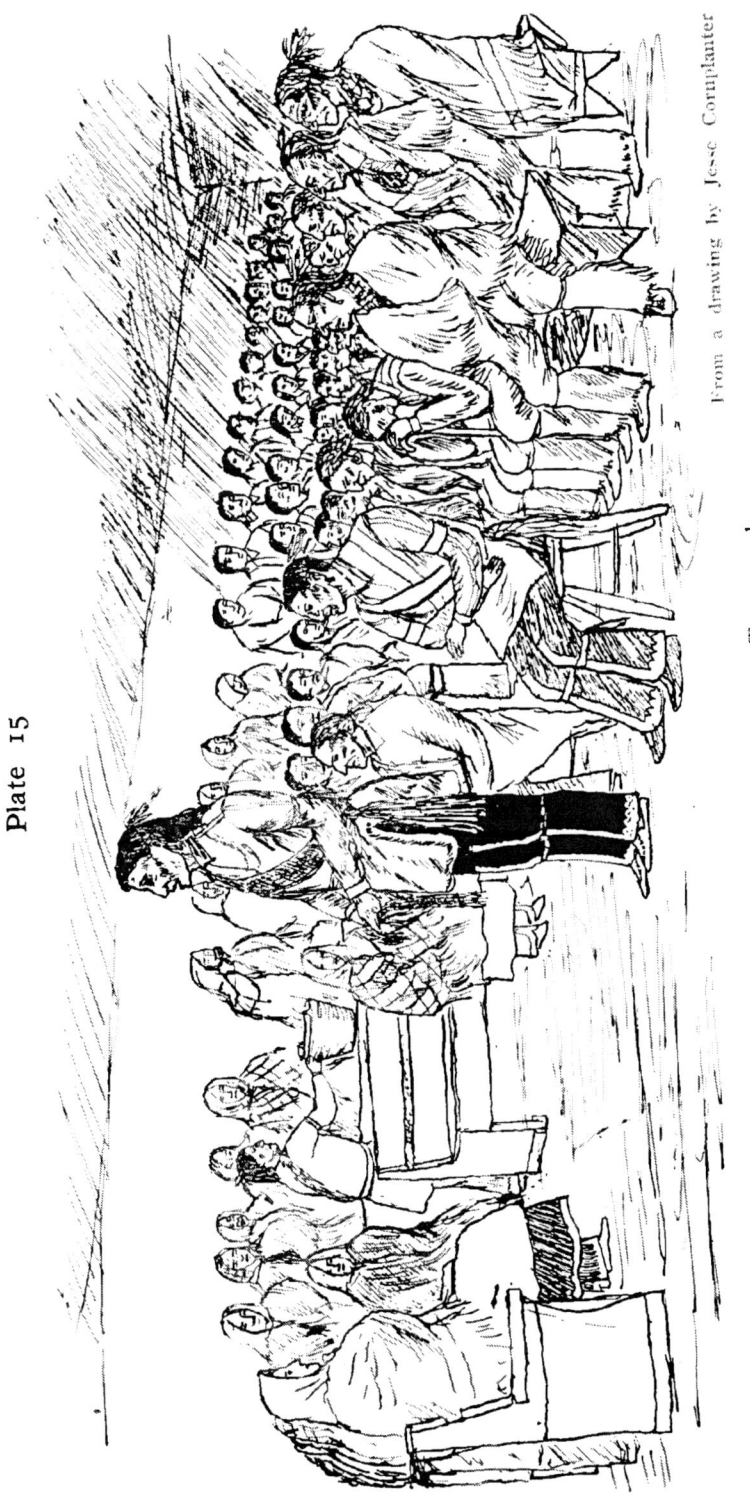

Handsome Lake preaching at Tonawanda

From a drawing by Jesse Cornplanter

"Then answered the messengers, 'What you say is true. The man was the punisher and his delight is to see people filled with strong drink.'"

So they said and he said. Eniaiehuk.

THE JOURNEY OVER THE GREAT SKY-ROAD

SECTION 82

"'Now another message.

"'Now it is the time for our departure. We shall now go on a journey and then you shall see the coming of the fourth messenger, the journey of our friends and the works of the living of earth. More, you will see the house of the punisher and the lands of our Creator.'"

So they said. Eniaiehuk.

SECTION 83

"'Now another message.

"Suddenly as they looked, a road slowly descended from the south sky[1] and came to where they were standing. Now thereon he saw the four tracks of the human race going in one direction. The footprints were all of different sizes from small to great. Now moreover a more brilliant light than the light of earth appeared."

So they said. Eniaiehuk.

SECTION 84

"'Now they said unto him, 'We will tarry here a while in order that you may see.'

"Now as he watched and believed, he saw a large woman sitting there. Now the woman was grasping frantically at all things within her reach, and it seemed that she could not stand because of her great size. That was what he saw.

"Then they said to him, 'What did you see?'

"He answered, 'It is hard to say. I saw a woman sitting and she was large of size and snatching at everything about her. I am of the opinion that she can not rise.' So he answered when he spoke.

"Then the messengers answered, 'It is true. That which you saw was the evil of stinginess. She can not stand and thus she will

---

[1] The great sky-road of the Gai'wiio' is the milky way. The souls of the dead are supposed to journey over the broad band and divide at the forks. The multitude of stars are thought to be the footprints of the dead.

remain forever. Thus it will be with those who forsake religious teachings and think more of the things of earth than of the new world above. (Having glutted themselves with the things of earth they are unable to stand upon the heaven road.)'"[1]

So they said and he said. Eniaiehuk.

SECTION 85

"Now they said, 'We shall proceed.' Now the farther they went the more brilliant the light became. They had not gone far when the four messengers said, 'Now we will stop again. Look attentively at what you see.'

"So he looked and saw three groups of people and each group was of a different size. The first was large, the second small and the third still smaller.

"Then the messengers asked him, 'What do you see?'

"He answered, 'I saw three groups, the first a large group, the second half as large as the first and the third still smaller.' That is what he said when he answered.

"Then they replied, 'Truly you have seen. The groups represent the people of earth. The first group you saw was composed of those who have not repented; the second group was inclined half way, and the third group, the smallest one, was composed of those who have repented. They are protected by the true belief in Gai'wiio'.'"

So they said and he said. Eniaiehuk.

SECTION 86

"So they proceeded a short distance and again came to a halt. Then the messengers pointed out a spot and bade him watch attentively. Then he saw a house strongly built and within it he saw three different things. The first was a pair of handcuffs, the second a whip and the third a hang-rope."

"Then asked the messengers, 'What did you see?'

"He answered, 'The house I saw was strongly built and within the house I saw three different things. The first was a pair of handcuffs, the second a whip and the third a hangman's rope.' So he answered.

---

[1] Those who gain great riches and lack humility can not stand upon the sky-road nor can they walk. The poor and meek only can travel skyward and not even the poor unless their ways have been humble and marked with virtue. Thus it is said, "It is better to be poor on earth and rich in the sky-world than to have earth riches and no heaven."

"Then they replied, 'Truly it is a strongly built house. It is a prison. Now it is true that three things are there for punishment. How hard it is for a transgressor to see that he should be punished; yet it is the cry of the people that the laws of the white man are better than the teachings of Gai'wiio'. This frightens even the Great Spirit for he knows the punishment of those who say such things.'"

So they said and he said. Eniaiehuk.

SECTION 87

"So they proceeded and it was not long before they said, 'We must stop here.' Then they pointed in a certain direction and commanded him to watch. So he watched and as he did he saw a house with a spire and a path leading into the house and none out. There was no door, neither were there any windows in the house. Within was a great noise, wailing and crying, and the house was hot.

"Then the messengers asked him what he saw.

"He answered, 'I saw a house with a spire and a path leading to the house. There was no door, neither were there any windows in the house. Within was a great noise, wailing and crying, and the house was hot.'

"Then they replied, 'You have truly seen. It is a hard matter for Indians to embrace these conditions, that is, to embrace the belief of Bible believers.'"

So they said and he said. Eniaiehuk.

SECTION 88

"So they proceeded and had not gone far when the messengers said, 'Look downward upon the Buffalo Creek reservation.'

"Se he looked and the place seemed honeycombed and covered with a net.

"Then the messengers asked him what he saw.

"He answered, 'I saw the Buffalo Creek reservation and it seemed honeycombed like ice and covered with a net.' So he replied.

"Then the messengers said, 'Truly! We think that this reservation will fall.' Now they said moreover that it was the duty of the chiefs to preserve it but it should be hard for some should take an upper hand.'"

So they said and he said. Eniaiehuk.

SECTION 89

"So they proceeded a little ways farther and soon they said, 'We will stop here.' Then they pointed out a certain spot and said, 'Watch! Look upon the eastern heavens and observe!'

"So he looked and saw two immense drops (or balls of liquid) hanging, one red and one yellow. It seemed that they were suspended only for an instant and would momentarily fall.

"Then the messengers asked, 'What did you see there?'

"He answered, 'I saw two drops, one red and one yellow, suspended as if about to fall.'

"Then the messengers replied, 'Truly you have spoken. It is so. Should one of those drops fall it would bring great calamity upon the earth. Many people would leave the earth should one drop but we are doing our utmost to prevent such an event.'"

So they said and he said. Eniaiehuk.

SECTION 90

"So they proceeded but had not gone a long distance before they said, 'We will stop and watch a certain place. Now listen to the earth.'

"So he listened and as well as he could understand he thought that he heard wailing and mourning. The sounds seemed to be the crying of children.

"Then the messengers asked, 'What did you observe?'

"He answered, 'I thought that I heard the wailing of the aged and the crying of children.'

"Then the messengers replied, 'It is true. What you have heard is the substance of life going back to the Creator. When this time comes there will be great misery upon the earth.'"

So they said and he said. Eniaiehuk.

SECTION 91

"So they proceeded a little ways farther and in a short time they reached a certain spot and stopped.

"Then said the messengers, 'Look toward the setting sun.'

"So he looked and saw. Now as he looked he seemed to see a man pacing to and fro. He seemed to be a white man and in his hand he seemed to have a bayonet with which he prodded the ground. Now moreover he seemed very angry.

"Then said the messengers, 'What did you see?'

"He answered, 'I saw what seemed to be a man pacing to and fro. He seemed to be a white man and in his hand he seemed to have a bayonet with which he prodded the ground, and, moreover, it seemed that he was angry.' So he said when he answered.

"Then the messengers said, 'It is true. He is a white man and in a temper. It is true. Indians must not help him and the head-men must honestly strive to prevent their followers from helping him.' "[1]

So they said and he said. Eniaiehuk.

SECTION 92

" So they proceeded on their journey and had not gone far when they stopped.

" Then the messengers said, ' Watch attentively.' Then they pointed out to him a certain spot midway between the earth and the clouds. So he watched there. Now this is true. He saw a house suspended there and on the veranda with a railing about it, a man walked and with him was a penny dog (kwĕn'nĭs djĭ''yä). Now moreover the man was rejoicing and he was a white man.

" Then said the messengers, ' What did you see?'

" He answered, ' I saw a house suspended in the air and on the porch with a railing about it a man was walking and with him was a penny dog. Now moreover the man was a white man.'

" Then the messengers said, ' Truly you have seen. It is said that the man is the first and oldest president of the United States. Now he enjoys himself and he is the only white man so near the new world of our Creator. Now it is said that there was once a time when the Thirteen Fires and the King[2] were in trouble. The Thirteen Fires were victorious and this man won the victory from the king. Said the king, " You have overpowered me, so now I release everything that was in my control, even these Iroquois who were my helpers. It rests with you what shall be done with them. Let them be to you a thing for a sacrifice." Then said the president, " I shall let them live and go back to the places that are theirs for they are an independent people." So it is said. Now this man did a great work. He has ordered things that we may enjoy ourselves, as long as the sun shines and waters run. This is the doing of our Great Creator.' "[3]

So they said and he said. Eniaiehuk.

---

[1] This section refers to the " war in the west," probably General Harrison's campaign against Tecumseh in 1811. Red Jacket and all the principal chiefs were anxious to preserve peace and did all within their power to prevent their young warriors from enlisting on either side but were not entirely successful. The issue was of such moment that the prophet deemed it wise to reveal the will of the four messengers in the matter.

[2] The word here is feminine and should be translated queen but this would manifestly not be in accord with truth. The error was made by Chief John Jacket who wrote out the Gai'wiio' in Seneca in 1860, during the reign of Queen Victoria.

[3] See Washington and the Iroquois, p 137.

SECTION 93

"So then they proceeded on their journey but had not gone far when they stopped.

"Then the messengers said, 'Watch,' and pointed to a certain spot toward the setting sun.

"So he watched and saw a large object revolving. It was white and moving slowly.

"Then said the four messengers, 'What did you see?'

"He answered, 'I saw a large object revolving. It was white and moving slowly.'

"Then said the messengers, 'It is true. The thing is that which regulates the air over the earth. It is that which we call the Odā'eo (the veil over all). It is said that it would bring great calamity should it revolve too fast. Should it turn faster it would injure mankind. Now we are the regulators and watchers of the veil over all.'"

So they said and he said. Eniaiehuk.

SECTION 94

"So they proceeded on their journey and it happened that a vision appeared unto them. They seemed to be advancing toward an approaching man. Soon they met him and passed. Now when they were a distance apart they turned and he was facing them. So they greeted each other. Then said the man, 'Sedwāgo'wanĕ, I must ask you a question. Did you never hear your grandfathers say that once there was a certain man upon the earth across the great waters who was slain by his own people?' That was what he said when he spoke.

"Then answered Sedwāgo'wanĕ, 'It is true. I have heard my grandparents say this.'

"Then answered the man, 'I am he.' (Segaⁿ'hedŭs, *He who resurrects*). And he turned his palms upward and they were scarred and his feet were likewise and his breast was pierced by a spear wound. It appeared that his hands and his feet were torn by iron nails.

"All this was true. It could be seen and blood was fresh upon him.

"Then said the man, 'They slew me because of their independence and unbelief. So I have gone home to shut the doors of heaven that they may not see me again until the earth passes away. Then will all the people cry to me for succor, and when I come it will be in this wise: my face will be sober and I shall turn it to my people. Now let me ask how your people receive your teachings.'

"He answered, 'It is my opinion that half my people are inclined to believe in me.'

"Then answered he, 'You are more successful than I for some believe in you but none in me. I am inclined to believe that in the end it will also be so with you. Now it is rumored that you are but a talker with spirits (djīs'gäⁿdătăha·[1]). Now it is true that I am a spirit and the one of him who was murdered. Now tell your people that they will become lost when they follow the ways of the white man.'"

So that is what he said. Eniaiehuk.

SECTION 95

"So they proceeded on their journey and had not gone far when they came to a halt.

"Then the messengers pointed out a certain spot and said, 'Watch attentively,' and beheld a man carrying loads of dirt and depositing them in a certain spot. He carried the earth in a wheelbarrow and his task was a hard one. Then he knew that the name of the man was Sagoyewat'ha, a chief.

"Then asked the messengers, 'What did you see?'

"He answered, 'I beheld a man carrying dirt in a wheelbarrow and that man had a laborious task. His name was Sagoyewat'ha, a chief.'

"Then answered the messengers, 'You have spoken truly. Sagoyewat'ha is the name of the man who carries the dirt. It is true that his work is laborious and this is for a punishment for he was the one who first gave his consent to the sale of Indian reservations. It is said that there is hardship for those who part with their lands for money or trade. So now you have seen the doom of those who repent not. Their eternity will be one of punishment.'"[2]

So they said and he said. Eniaiehuk.

---

[1] See Spiritism, p. 126.

[2] The followers of the Gai'wiio' to this day mention the name of Red Jacket with contempt. While they acknowledge his mental superiority they have no other admiration for him. He was ever the enemy of Cornplanter and Ganiodaiio with whom he had frequent collision and recognized the sachem-prophet only as an impostor. The teachings of Ganiodaiio have done much to prejudice the Iroquois against Red Jacket.

SECTION 96

"Now again they took up their journey and had not traveled far when they saw a crowd on both sides of the road. And when they came to where it was they saw that they were at the forks of the road. One road, on the right, was a narrow one and the tracks upon it were mostly those of children and all were pointed in one direction. Few adults had their tracks on this road, the road rough and wide. Now as they watched they saw a woman approaching the forks of the road from behind them. She came to where the road divided and as she halted before the roads a man who stood to the left shouted, ' To this side.' (Now the road of the wicked is owa'ĕtgäⁿ, a rough road.) Then the man on the right said, ' Not so. This woman has done her whole duty. She has truly repented.' Then answered the man on the left, ' You are wrong, for her repentance has been of short duration and so of slight effect. But the man on the right replied, ' Truly in her earth-life she repented and was faithful to her promises. This is all that is required and she will walk upon the narrow road.'

"Now one of the messengers turned to him and said, ' The woman has lived a repented life for three days and has entered into the happy eternity. It was not an easy matter for her to do so of herself, but we, the messengers, have plead before the Creator and he has heard us. Three times we assist every one who believes to continue in the faith of the Gai'wiio'. At this division in the great road we guide the spirits of the earth into Tain'tciadĕ (heaven land). At the forks of the road the spirits of the dead are divided. The narrow road leads to the pleasant lands of the Creator and the wide and rough road leads to the great lodge of the punisher.'"

So they said and he said. Eniaiehuk.

SECTION 97

"So now another.

"' Verily you have seen the breast of a man hanging here by the road and in the center of that breast you saw a bullet hole.[1] Now we have caused this thing to be placed there. All will see it and he will see it who did the wrong when he comes upon the great road and know that he must turn aside and enter upon a journey over the wide and rough road.'"

So they said and he said. Eniaiehuk.

---

[1] See section 56.

SECTION 98

"Now again they told him that they would take up their journey and as they went they drew near to the house of the punisher. As they went over the broad road they walked well on the sides for the path was very stony. Now, strange, this was true; some great force seemed pushing them onward toward the house of the punisher.[1] Soon they began to inhale heated air and soon they heard the far away echoes of mournful cries borne on the blasts of the hot wind. At times the air was suffocating and the cries of the doomed were distressing."

So he said. Eniaiehuk.

SECTION 99

"Now they approached a great lodge. It seemed constructed of iron that had been highly heated and allowed to cool. Within the building hot vapor was rising from the fire pits.

"Now the messengers spoke saying, 'Let us tarry here a while.' Then one of the beings took from his bosom a crystal and pointed it at the lodge. He approached holding the glass at arm's length and as he came near the lodge arose to the height of the man so powerful was the crystal." Eniaiehuk.

SECTION 100

"Now they saw and then everyone knew that the house was very long and extended far out of the eye's reach. Now this is true. When a certain woman within saw the four and him drawing near she stretched out her arms and cried for help. Then answered the four, 'It is beyond our power to alter your condition now. Our work was with you on earth. Too late.'"

So they said and he said. Eniaiehuk.

SECTION 101

"Now as they looked they saw a being walking about as if he were the master of the lodge. He seemed continually distorting himself. At times horns shot out from his forehead, at times a cloven foot appeared and at times a tail was visible.[2]

---

[1] The prophet here alludes to the ease with which one may glide over the broad road. "It is no work to sin," says the preacher, "for the devil furnishes the legs for you."

[2] The prophet has very evidently borrowed his devil from transatlantic sources.

" Then said the four messengers to Ganiodai'io'. ' That being is the punisher. It is he who torments those who have refused the words of Gai'wiio' when they heard them on the earth.' "

So they said. Eniaiehuk.

SECTION 102

" In a loud voice the punisher cried to a certain person saying, ' Come hither.' The punisher held a drinking vessel in his hand and within it was molten metal and thrusting it in the hands of the man he had called he said, ' Now warm yourself again as was your custom while on the earth for you loved hot drink.' Now the man pleaded but the punisher compelled him to swallow the molten metal. Then the man screamed in a loud voice and fell prone upon the ground with vapor steaming from his throat. Now he cried no more.

" Then said the four messengers, ' You have seen the manner of punishing those who persist in taking the fiery drink.' "

So they said. Eniaiehuk.

SECTION 103

" Now as they looked the master of the house spoke saying, ' Come.' Now the master knew the name of every one within the house. And straightway a woman came to where he stood. Then he grabbed her and forced her body into a great cauldron filled with a boiling liquid. Frequently he looked down into the cauldron to see if the woman had come again to the top. Suddenly she shot to the surface crying in a strange voice like some unknown animal and then sank down again. Soon again she appeared and cried, ' O, it is too hot! I should have an interval in which to cool myself!' Answered the punisher, ' Thou are not one-minded,' and jerking her out he flung her on one side. But the woman screeched in agony, ' O, it is too cold!' and her complaint was continuous and she moaned, ' It is too cold!' Then the punisher thrust her back into the boiling cauldron and immediately her bones rattled to the bottom. Such was the punishment given by the keeper of the house of torment.

" Then spoke the four messengers and said, ' This is the punishment given those who practice witchcraft. The woman whom you saw will suffer two deaths in this place and when her body is reduced to dust the punisher will gather them up again and conjure the dust back into a living body and continue his sport until finally he has become weary when he will blow her ashes to destruction. Such things happen to those who will not believe in Gai'wiio'.'"

So they said and he said. Eniaiehuk.

SECTION 104

"Now he saw a certain nude woman coming out from a crowd and in all the hair of her body were writhing serpents. Her cheeks were parched to the bone where she had been wont to color them and likewise where her hair was parted there was no flesh. Now she was greatly ashamed but she could not cover her nakedness. So in this condition he saw her.

"Then said the four messengers, 'Saw thou that woman? In life she was wont to give on'oityi'yĕnde, [secret powders] to men to attract them to her. So you have seen the punishment meted out to those who do this and do not repent.'"

So they said. Eniaiehuk.

SECTION 105

"Now they revealed another.

"Now the master of the house looked about and saw another person. So he said, 'Come here, my nephew, I wish to see you flog your wife as was your custom on the earth.' The punisher then pointed out the image of a woman heated hot with fire and commanded the man to beat the image. Then the man pleaded with moans to be released from the command but the punisher forced him to strike the image with his bare hands, and the man fell in agony prostrate upon the floor screaming. So he saw.

"Then said the four messengers, 'You have seen the punishment given to the man who beat his wife. Thus it will be with all who fail to repent and fail to believe in Gai'wiio'. Now such was the evil that this man did to grieve his Creator.'"

So they said and he said. Eniaiehuk.

SECTION 106

"Now they revealed another.

"The master of the house called out the names of two persons, saying, 'Come here, my nephews,'[1] and straightway they stood before him. Then said he, 'Commence an argument, you two, for you are the man and wife who in your earth-life were wont to

---

[1] The Seneca term means, "my sister's children," thus both nephews and nieces.

quarrel continually, so quarrel again!' Then when he saw that the people were reluctant he compelled them to argue. Then they disputed until their eyes bulged from their heads, their tongues lolled out and flames of fire shot from ganä'shoo'. So this was what he saw.

"Then said the messengers, 'This is the punishment reserved for those who quarrel without ceasing and fail to repent.'"

So they said. Eniaiehuk.

SECTION 107

"Now they showed him another.

"Now the punisher called out a certain woman's name saying, 'Come to me, my niece,' and straightway she came. Then said he, 'It was once your delight gaknowe'haat.' As he said this he lifted up an object from a pile and thrust it within her. Now the object was like ha'ji'no' gänää", and it was red hot. Then she cried aloud in agony and she fell with steam issuing from her body. Now there were three piles of gä'nää', the first white, the second red and the third black and all were gä'nää'.' So this was what he saw.

"Then the messengers said, 'You have seen the punishment of the immoral woman.'"

So they said. Eniaiehuk.

SECTION 108

"Now they showed him another.

"Now the punisher called out in a loud voice saying, 'My nephew, come hither,' and the man stood before him. 'Now, nephew, play your violin as was once your delight.' The punisher handed the man a bar of hot iron and forced him to rub it upon his arm. So he played and the cords of his arm were the strings of the instrument and made the music. So in great agony he cried and screamed until he fell.[1]

"Then said the four messengers, 'You have seen the punishment of the man who failed to repent.'"

So they said. Eniaiehuk.

SECTION 109

"Now they revealed another.

"Now the punisher called out in a loud voice and commanded two persons to appear before him. Now when they stood before

---

[1] The pagan Indians detest the "fiddle" and "fiddle dances" as things of great evil and assert that they produce as much wickedness as drunkenness.

him he handed them what seemed a pack of red hot iron cards. Then he forced the two to sit down facing each other and compelled them to shuffle the cards and as they did flames spurted out from between them. So they cried out in great agony, sucked their fingers in their mouths, handled the cards again until their flesh was eaten away and the meat fell off. So this is what he saw.

"Then the messengers said, 'This is the punishment meted out to those who handle cards and repent not.'"

So they said. Eniaiehuk.

SECTION 110

"Verily he saw those who were upon the earth and those who were alive and he saw the wicked in the house of torment. He saw Gowono^n'gowa [she great talker], Găkon'go' [she-glutton animal], Gănonjoni'yon [hanging kettle] and Hano'ēs [head-eater]. Verily he saw these four persons.

"Then said the four messengers, 'These four have committed the great sin and can not be forgiven.'"

So they said. Eniaiehuk.

SECTION 111

"Then said the messengers, 'We will proceed on our journey. It would be a hard thing should we tarry too long and meet the Creator on the road before we reach his pleasant lands. If we should meet him you should be compelled to stay here forever.'"[1]

So they said. Eniaiehuk.

SECTION 112

"Then they went out upon the narrow road and had not gone far upon it when a far more brilliant light appeared. It was then that they smelled the fragrant odors of the flowers along the road. Delicious looking fruits were growing on the wayside and every kind of bird flew in the air above them. The most marvelous and beautiful things were on every hand. And all these things were on the heaven road." Eniaiehuk.

SECTION 113

"So they continued on their journey and after a short time they came to a halt. Then spoke the messengers, 'This place is called, "the spring" and it is a place for rest.' Then behold he saw the spring and he thought that he had never seen so beautiful and

---

[1] See legend, Two brothers who went to the sky, p. 132.

clear a fount of water. Then said the four, ' This is a place of refreshment.' One of the four drew a bottle from his bosom, so it seemed and it was, and dipped it in the spring. Then he said, ' You must partake first,' and so he took it, but when he looked at it he thought it was not enough. So he said, ' I think that this is not sufficient.' And when he had said this the messengers looked at one another and smiled and one said, ' Truly it is enough. If it lacks, there is still the spring and the vessel may be refilled. So all took and drank and all the drink that all wished was in the bottle. Then said the messengers, ' This is a place of meeting. Now we will go on our journey.' " [There are also said to have been two other meeting places, Diogē″djaie, Grassy Place, and Dion′dot, The Tree.]

So they said. Eniaiehuk.

SECTION 114

" So then they proceeded on their journey and had gone but a short way when they saw someone coming toward them and it was not long before they met. Then he saw it was a dog and when they met, the dog began to wag its tail and sprang upon him. Then he recognized the animal as his own dog and it appeared just as it had when he had decorated it for the sacrifice in the Hadidji′yontwŭs [New Year's ceremony]. Then said the four, ' This thing attests to the value of our thankoffering to the Creator.' "[1]

So they said. Eniaiehuk.

SECTION 115

" So they took up their journey again and in a short time came to a halt. In the distance before them a man appeared to be coming and soon he came nearer. Then he saw that the man was guiding two others, one on either side of him. Now as he looked he saw that one was the daughter of Gaiänt′wakä and it appeared that she was a large child. With her was his (Ganio′dai′io') own son, an infant, and they greeted one another, the son and the daughter. Now one could see that they were not strangers for they were friendly. Now moreover a fourth person was leading them all."
Eniaiehuk.

SECTION 116

" Now that person spoke and said, ' I brought them with me to testify to the truth that those of the lower world when they pass away come hither.'

---

[1] See p. 85, Sacrifice of the white dog.

"Then spoke the daughter of Gaiän'twakă, 'I send a message. It is this: It grieves me to know that my brothers on the earth disagree with my father. Bid them cease their disagreement.' So she said."

Eniaiehuk.

SECTION 117

"So they took up their journey again and in a short time came to a halt. There was a more brilliant light and as they stood suddenly they heard the echo of a commanding voice calling the people together for the performance of the great feather dance.

"Then asked the four messengers, 'What think you has happened?'

"He answered, 'I heard the commanding voice of Joi'ise calling the people to celebrate the great feather dance.'

"Then replied the four messengers, 'Verily, Joi'ise, your friend is he who calls. He it was who was faithful and good and when he passed away in the lands of the Creator he continued as on the earth [to be a leader].'"

So they said. Eniaiehuk.

SECTION 118

"So they took up their journey again and after a ways the four messengers said, 'We have arrived at the point where you must return. Here there is a house prepared for your eternal abode but should you now enter a room you could never go back to the earth-world.'"

So they said. Eniaiehuk.

SECTION 119

"Now when he arrived in Tonawanda having come from Dionoⁿ'sădegĕ he was reluctant in performing his religious duties."

SECTION 120

"Now he was at Cornplanter ten years, at Cold Spring two years and at Tonawanda four years. From there he went to Ganonktiyuk'gegäo, Onondaga, and there fell our head man."

SECTION 121

"Now it happened that while he still abode at Tonawanda an invitation was extended by the people of Onondaga asking him to come and preach Gai'wiio' to the chiefs and head men there."

SECTION 122

"Now it happened that the four messengers appeared to him when the invitation was extended, they the four speakers and messengers of the Great Spirit of the worlds.

"Now the first words that they spoke were these, 'They have stretched out their hands pleading for you to come and they are your own people at Onondaga. Let this be the way, prepare yourself and cleanse your body with medicine.[1] It is necessary moreover for you to secrete yourself in some hidden spot and await our call to start.'"

So they said. Eniaiehuk.

SECTION 123

"Now there will be another and his name will be the New Voice, Hawĕnose".

"So now it was that Ganio'dai'io' was bidden the third time to sing his song and this the messengers said would be the last.

"Now then he said, 'There is nothing to incumber me from fulfilling my call.'"

So said our head man. Eniaiehuk.

SECTION 124

"Thus it happened in the past and it is the truth.

"'I must now take up my final journey to the new world,' he thought, and he was greatly troubled and longed for the home of his childhood and pined to return.

---

[1] Purification. The herb used most extensively by the Iroquois for "purification" was witch hopple, the bark of which was used both as an emetic and a purgative. For an emetic the bark was peeled upward and for a purgative downward.

Early in the spring during the spell of warm days the people would take their kettles, jars of soup and deerskins and go alone into the woods for their ceremony of purification. Here they would scrape the bark, build a fire and make a strong infusion of the witch hopple bark. The drink was taken in large quantities and then the Indian would sit wrapped in his deerskin to await the results. From sunrise to sunset the drink would be taken until the alimentary tract was completely emptied. Toward sundown a little soup would be sipped to ward off excessive weakness, and give strength to return home. The next morning sweat baths were often taken, though not always, and then solid food was eaten. This process was thought to purify the body and without doubt did much to do so. Besides the customary spring purification others were sometimes ordered for disease and for preparations for ordeals, tests and ceremonial purposes. The process was again repeated in the autumn.

"Then came the four messengers to him and said, 'The children will comfort you in your distress for they are without sin. They will elect a certain one from among them to plead that you continue to abide among them.'"

So they said. Eniaiehuk.

"Now it happened that it came to pass that all the children assembled and their spokesman did his utmost to exact a promise from Ganio'dai'io'. So great was his grief that after he had spoken a short time he could no longer plead. Then another boy was appointed by the children, a boy not bashful but rough and bold. So he, too, endeavored to persuade Ganio'dai'io', but it was a difficult task for him and he could scarcely speak, but he did. Then Ganio'dai'io' made an answer to the children. He rose and exhorted them to ever be faithful and a great multitude heard him and wept." Eniaiehuk.

SECTION 125

"Now at this time there was a man and his name was New Voice, a chief of equal rank with Cornplanter. Now this man urged Ganio'dai'io' to accept the invitation of his friends and relatives of Onondaga. He said, 'It is as if they were stretching forth their necks to see you coming. Now I am going forth to a gathering of chiefs at Buffalo on the long strip that is the fireplace of the Six Nations,[1] the great meeting place of human creatures. I will go so that I may believe that you are on your journey and I will ride away as fast as my horse can go.' So he said."

SECTION 126

"Now then Ganio'dai'io' started on his journey and a large number followed him that they might hear him speak. They had no conveyances but traveled afoot.

"Now when they came to their camping spot at Ganowa'gĕs,[2] he said to them in a commanding voice, 'Assemble early in the morning.' Now when they did he offered thanks and afterward he said, 'I have had a dream, a wondrous vision. I seemed to see a pathway, a trail overgrown and covered with grass so that it appeared not to have been traveled in a long time.' Now no one spoke but

---

[1] At this time there was an Onondaga village on the Buffalo Creek tract. It became therefore a legal meeting place for the Six Nations. The Canadian refugees often returned to council there.

[2] The site of the village opposite the present Avon, N. Y.

when all had heard and he had finished they dispersed and they continued on their journey."

SECTION 127

" Now their next camping spot was near Ganŭndase"ge'.[1]

" Now when they had all come up to the spot he called out in a commanding voice, ' Come hither and give thanks.' Now when the ceremony was over he said, ' I heard in a dream a certain woman speaking but I am not able to say whether she was of Onondaga or of Tonawanda from whence we came.' So this was what he said when he related his dream. Then all the company dispersed." Eniaiehuk.

SECTION 128

" So they proceeded on their journey.

" Now it happened that when they were near the reservation line he said, ' Let us refresh ourselves before going farther.' So they sat down and ate and then they continued on their journey."

" Now it happened that when they were over the reservation line that he said, ' I have forgotten my knife. I may have left it where we stopped and ate last. I can not lose that knife for it is one that I prize above many things. Therefore I must return and find it.'

" The preacher went back alone and there was no one to go with him. Now he became very ill and it was with great difficulty that he returned. The others had all gone on to the council but he was not able to get to it for he was very sick and in great distress. So when he did not come it was said, ' Our meeting is only a gathering about the fireplace.' " Eniaiehuk.

SECTION 129

" Now it happened that they all wished to comfort him. So for his pleasure they started a game of lacrosse[2] and played the game well. It was a bright and beautiful day and they brought him out so that he might see the play. Soon he desired to be taken back into the house." Eniaiehuk.

SECTION 130

" Now shortly after he said a few words. To the numbers gathered about him to hear his message he said, ' I will soon go to

---

[1] The Seneca village near the present site of Geneva, N. Y.
[2] Games were often played to cheer and cure the sick. Special foods were given the players.

my new home.[1] Soon I will step into the new world for there is a plain pathway before me leading there. Whoever follows my teachings will follow in my footsteps and I will look back upon him with outstretched arms inviting him into the new world of our Creator. Alas, I fear that a pall of smoke will obscure the eyes of many from the truth of Gai'wiio' but I pray that when I am gone that all may do what I have taught.'

"This is what he said. This is what Ganio'dai'io', our head man, said to his people." Eniaiehuk.

[Then the preacher says:] "Relatives and friends: His term of ministry was sixteen years. So preached our head man, Ganio'dai'io'.

"Let this be our thanks to you and to the four messengers also. I give thanks to them for they are the messengers of our Creator. So, also, I give thanks to him whom we call Sĕdwāgowănĕ, our great teacher. So, also, I give thanks to our great Creator.

"So have I said, I, Sosondowa (Great Night), the preacher."

[Signed]   EDWARD CORNPLANTER, *Sosondowa*

---

[1] Handsome Lake died August 10, 1815, at Onondaga. His last moments were spent in a small cabin near the creek that runs into Onondaga creek at the foot of the terrace. Three persons attended him and swore to keep all details secret. He is said to have died before his nephew, Henry Obeal, could reach him.

PART 2

FIELD NOTES ON THE RITES AND CEREMONIES OF THE GANIO'DAI'O' RELIGION[1]

GÄNÄ'YASTA'

The midwinter festival of the Iroquois, commonly called Indian New Year.

On the third day of what the Seneca term Niskowŭkni ne'' Sadē'goshä or the moon of midwinter, a council of head men is called and officers elected to officiate at the Gänä'yasta' or midwinter thanksgiving ceremony to be held two days later. Officers are chosen from each of the two brotherhoods[2] of clans.

On the first day of the ceremony officers called Ondeyä, dressed in buffalo skins, meet and lay out a route of houses which each pair of Ondeyä is to visit. This settled, they draw the buffalo heads over their heads and start out.

There are three excursions of Ondeyä from their lodges, one at about 9 a. m., one at about 12 m. and one at about 3 p. m. Two Ondeyä, carrying corn pounders painted with red stripes, knock at the door of a house and entering intone:

Hail, nephews. Now also the cousins with you. Now also you see the big heads.

>Ye hē! Gwäwandē!
>Oneⁿ''dĭq wodewē'noyē ne' nē'sēso gwäwandē!
>Oneⁿ''dĭq īswāgēⁿ' noīwane'!

This is repeated and the Ondeyä depart.

At noon the Ondeyä repair to their meeting place and emerging again go over the same route. Their message as they enter a lodge at this time is:

Hail. Be clean! Do not be confused, O nephews. Do not tread upon things, nephews, cousins, when you move.

>Yēhe! Jokwchon! sänon'di gwä'wandī! danondodādē, gwä'wandī nene'sēso nänondo''yäno'!

At 3 p. m., returning to the same lodge, the message is:

>Yēhē! Oiseⁿdase' susniun'nano ne'' swaisē'' dūgayio' sändo.'
>One'' dĭq ītchigaine'soⁿ nongwŭk'sado' nenwande' sä'noⁿ dĭq ītch'nonadoktē' ongwŭkädo'. One'' dĭq někho'' non'jiyē.

---

[1] Taken at Newtown, Cattaraugus reservation, January 1905, by A. C. Parker.

[2] See Phratries.

[81]

After one has intoned this message or announcement the other pokes up the ashes with a basswood paddle and sings a song.

The first day is spent in this way, formal announcements being given by the officers.

On the morning of the second day all the lodges are visited by officers called Hadēiyäyo'. Later, say 9 a. m., clan officers, known as Hanä'sishĕ, begin their round of visits. Two men and two women are chosen from the phratries and going in couples to the various houses conduct a thanks or praise service. The burden of their words is a thanksgiving to God for the blessings that have been received by that house during the past year.

When this ceremony is over these officers throw up a paddle (Wadigusä'wea) signifying that the ceremony is over. At this time a chief makes a long thanksgiving speech in the council house.

At noon the "big feather" dancers visit every lodge and dance the sacred dance. Two women at least must participate. On entering a lodge the leader of the feather dancers must say:

Onĕⁿ"dĭq' hodo"issoin'yŭnde sedwä'ä'wŭk gäoⁿ'ya'ge' honoñ'ge'. Nēkho"nai' hodo'isshoⁿgoⁿoindi ne" häwoⁿn'. Hodawisa'sē' Osto'wägowă.

Onĕⁿ"dĭq'dji'wŭsnowät nĕ" gissäⁿ äyĕⁿoñgwē Osto'wägowă. Gagwēgoⁿ,' onĕᵘ" dĭq,' djiwŭsnowät heniyoⁿ' swao'iwayandoⁿ'!

Da'neho"!

At about 2 p. m. public dances begin in the "long house."

The Society of Bears, which during the early afternoon had been holding a session in the house of some member, enter the long house and dance publicly. The same is true of the False Face Company.

Other dances are the Pigeon song dance (Tcä'kowa) and the Gädä'ciot. The only dance in which physical contact is permitted is the Yĕndonïssontă' or "dance of the beans." Dancers hold each other's hands as they circle around the singers. This is to represent the bean vine as it clings to a sapling or corn stalk.

On the morning of the third day the priest arises before daylight and standing at the door of the council house begins his song of thanks. The song is sung until dawn appears and then the priest ceases. Should a fierce wind be blowing it is believed that when the words of the song float upward the Great Spirit will say, "Cease your movements, Oh wind, I am listening to the song of my children."

The first verse is as follows:

> Onĕⁿ'' dĭq' okno'wi, Onĕⁿ'' dĭq,' dasĕnni''dottondē
> Gäo'yä gütci'ja'! Yoändjä'gĕ igĕⁿ's
> Onĕⁿ'' dĭq' o'gai'wayi' onĕ''
> Dĕawĕn'nissĕ no'gowĕs
> Dĕowiono'gowes
> Saiwisa'honio'
> Onĕⁿ'' dĭq' wadi'wayēĭs.

The song begins with the singer's face to the west; he turns and sings in all directions, that all may hear his voice.

A legend relates that this song originated ages ago. An old woman is said to have been with child and before her son was born, from the heavens came this song.

Only one or two Indians sing this now, no others being able for some reason. After the song the priest calls upon the Great Spirit in these words:

> Ye, ye-e, yēē!
> Dane''agwa none''neⁿgä' nē'wa
> Onĕⁿ'' dĭq dasa''tondat' gäogĕ'gĕ'
> tci'ja', etc., etc.

At about 9 a. m. another officer of religion enters the long house and sings the Ganio'dai'io' song:

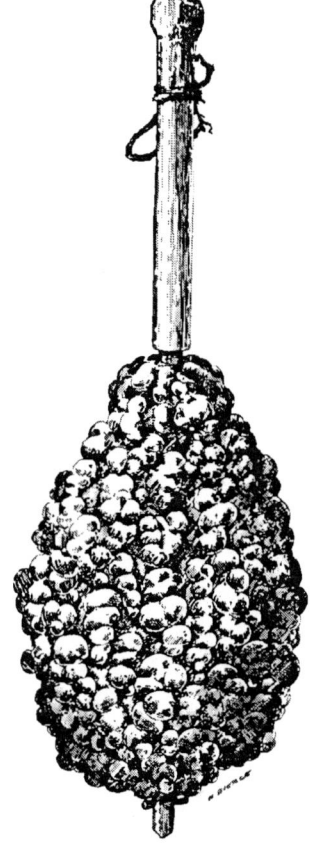

Fig. 1 Prayer rattle made from a dried squash. Allegany Seneca specimen.

Translation:

> I love my world, I love my time, I love my growing children. I love my old people, I love my ceremonies.

At noon various societies and companies which have been holding sessions in private lodges adjourn to the council house to engage in public ceremonies. The great feather dance is celebrated at noon. Afterward nearly all the common dances are given, among which is the woman's football game and dance.

The morning of the third day is greeted as the previous day, by the song and prayer of the priest.

At 9 a. m. of the fourth day the Gonio'dai'io' song is chanted again. Meanwhile the company of harvest dancers hold their dances at private houses going to the long house (ganoⁿ'sŭsgeⁿ') at noon. Soon after the Bird Society or Gane"gwäē enters the council house and begins its dance. Two dancers are chosen from each phratry, as are also two speakers. The evening is devoted to the Trotting, Fish, Pigeon, Bear, False Face, Buffalo and other dances. At 10 p. m. the ceremonies cease.

On the fifth day the dawn ceremony is repeated and at 9 a. m. the Ganio'dai'io' song is sung. Societies hold meetings in their own lodges.

At about 1 p. m. a company of women dancers visit each house, dance and sing and return to the long house. False Face beggars also roam from lodge to lodge in search of sacred tobacco. In the afternoon and evening various dances are held in the long house. At about 11 p. m. the Husk Face Company enters the long house and engages in their public ceremony. After this dance the people are dismissed by a chief.

Fig. 2 The Thanksgiving song

The morning of the sixth day is devoted to the dog sacrifice and the tobacco offering. Afterward the Adoⁿ'we' are sung. This song may be translated: I am now going home, I step upon another world, I turn and extend my arms for a friend to lead me, I pray all may go where I go. Now the earth is smoky and none can see the other world [as I do].

On the seventh day the Honon'diont hold a morning dance and then proceed to cook the feast. Costumed feather dancers enter the long house and dance. The " wind is open for names," or opportunity is now given to bestow names. At this point if a boy is to be named the priest rises and says, " Hio'gĕnē", dji'wagä ne-e!"

" Hu", hu", hu"hu"-ā!" respond the people.

If a girl is to be named there is no ceremony other than the mere announcement of the name. A speech is now made by a chief bidding people make ready for the sacred bowl game.

Honon'diont visit each lodge exacting from every person stakes for the sacred gamble. Each phratry is to play against the other The Honon'diont then meet and match articles, value for value.

The night previous every person endeavors to have a prophetic dream, whereby they may know the result of this game. No one must cheat in this game for " it is God's."

The great feather dance is repeated and names bestowed on this day. At night the Husk Faces return and give a grand final dance.

The ninth day is the last one of the midwinter's ceremony. Early in the morning the priest gives a thanksgiving " sermon." At 5 p. m. occurs the dance in honor of the " three sisters," Diohē"ko, (these-we-live-on). Afterward the woman's dance is held, alternating with the following men's dances, Trotting, Pumpkin, Pigeon and Beans. The feast is then distributed and the people disperse.

THE WHITE DOG SACRIFICE[1]

A preliminary translation of the ceremonial prayer at the burning of the white dog at the Seneca Indian new year's ceremony (February).

Wotokwaiiendakwa Gaiantguntgwaa

(wotok'waiïen'dakwa gaiänt'guntgwä')

Gwa! Gwa! Gwa!
So now this is the appointed time!
Oh listen, you who dwell in the sky!

---

[1] Recorded February 1906, at Cattaraugus reservation.

Our words are straight —
Only these can we speak unto you,
Oh you from whom we are descended,
Oh you who dwell in the sky!
You look down upon us and know that we are all children.
Now we petition you as we burn this sacred tobacco!
Now we commence our invocation,
Now we speak of all that you have created.
Now [in the beginning] you did think that men-beings should inherit the blessings of your creations,
For you did say, " Earth was my birthplace! "
Now we have spoken in this incense [throws tobacco upon the flames].
Oh now inhale the smoke, so listen to our words.
Now we commence, we are all that remain upon the earth.
You behold the places that once were filled but now are empty;
We were unable to change it for you made the law.
Now you think that there should be two conditions of temperature upon the earth;
One you thought should be cold and one should be warm
And when the warm season came that Diohē″ko, our substance, should spring from the bosom of Earth, our mother.
Now we have harvested the Diohe″ko from whence our living is
For the warm season has gone and we have here assembled.
Now we have made inquiries among all the people and they remember their promises,
For they promised you that they should assemble again at Gaiwanos'kwa gowa'
On the fifth sun of the moon Nĭskowŭk'nĭ.
So all fulfilled the plan and gathered together in the moon Nĭs'a, even those here present,
Oh you who were born of Earth, yet dwell in the sky!
Now all have fulfilled the law, for you did plan that the rites should be perpetuated even forever.
Now we are commencing, Oh you who were born of Earth!
Upon the first day the Great Feather dance went through the village for your pleasure.
The honon'diont and their cousins did their full duty.
Now on the next day Ganēo' was celebrated; at midday they went through the village,

And you did give us great joy because we performed this ceremony
For you did think that Ganëo' should be celebrated upon the earth for thine own self.
Thus did we fulfil your desires, Oh you who were born of Earth, yet live in the sky!
Now on the next day Gagandot was played.
Truly we did fulfil your desires,
Oh you who were born of Earth, you who live in the sky!
You did see all that was done,
Oh you who were born of Earth, you who live in the sky!
In the beginning you thought that you would lay this sacred tobacco by man's side
That men should have an incense with which to send his words up to the sky,
With which to lift his words when the year ended.
Truly we have fulfilled your desires and here we have that basket of sacred tobacco,
Oh you who were born of Earth, you who dwell in the sky!
[Throws tobacco on the flames.]
So now the smoke arises!
Oh inhale the incense as you listen!
For now do we commence to speak of what you have created.
In the beginning you thought that there should be a world
Upon which men beings should travel
That you might say, "They are my descendants."
Now there is a shaft that reaches up to you, Gancowi, the sacred song of the morning it is.
Now of your descendants as many as remain are gathered here.
Now you thought that there should be two sexes of men-beings,
That one should be the male and one should be the female,
And the function of the female should be the rearing of children.
Truly the females are fulfilling the design of their creation
For in their arms we see their children.
Truly it is in progress what you planned for them.
Now the smoke arises!
So now inhale this sacred incense!
Now we petition you that this thing should continue so henceforth,
And shall continue as long as the earth endures.
Now you thought that there should be a world
Upon which grasses of different kinds should grow

And that some should be medicinal,
And that some should yield fruits for a help to the men-beings who dwell upon the earth.
Thus did you think, O you who dwell in the sky!
Now it was ordered to be so when the warm season warmed the earth
And that it should be fulfilled them and that your descendants should see the return of things.
Now again the smoke arises
And the people speak through it to you,
Oh you who dwell in the sky!
Now we implore you that it may so occur again when the earth warms,
That your desires may be fulfilled and that your descendants may again see your creations.
Now again the smoke arises
And the people speak through it to you,
Oh you who dwell in the sky
Yet were born of Earth!

Now our sustenance you thought should be placed beside us,
And that men-beings should labor for their living.
These plans are all in progress
All see from whence their living comes.
Now we implore you that when the earth warms again that sustaining food may grow.
This we ask by the power of the incense tobacco,
Oh inhale it and listen to us,
Oh you, our great ancestor,
You who dwell in the sky!

You thought that there should be veins and that there should be fountains of water;
Now this thought is made a fact and is occurring
So we ask that this shall continue.
Now again the smoke arises
To you the father of all men-beings,
To you who dwell in the sky!

Now you thought that there should be living creatures,
Inhabiting the waters, useful to the people.

Now your thoughts have happened and we implore you that it may
   not be withdrawn,
Oh you who were born of Earth,
Oh you who dwell in the sky!
But may continue as long as earth endures.

So now another.
You did think that there should be world
And that bushes should grow upon it for a help to the people,
That the bushes should yield various fruits for the benefit of men-
   beings,
Oh you who were born of Earth,
Oh you who dwell in the sky,
May this continue as long as earth endures!

Now again the smoke arises,
Oh inhale the incense and continue to listen
Oh you who were born of Earth
Oh you who dwell in the sky!

So now another.
Now you did think that there should be forests upon the earth
And that they might be a help to the people.
So now moreover you did think that there should be a certain tree
That should yield sweet water from its trunk.
Now that tree is the Maple and it is faithful to its design
May this continue to be,
Oh you who dwell in the sky!

Now again the smoke arises,
And the people pray that this may still continue when the earth
   becomes warm again!
So now this thing is done.
Our words are as straight as we could make them.
Only this can we do for we are all young
Oh you who were born of Earth,
Oh you who dwell in the sky!
So now this one thing ends.

So now another.
You have created wild animals that roam in the forests,
You did think that they would be a pleasure to men-beings

Who should remember and say, "We are his descendants."
Now may they continue so to be,
Oh you who were born of Earth,
Oh you who dwell in the sky!

So now another.
The people are speaking;
They are continuing from the commencement of creation
Discussing those things that you didst think would be a benefit to men-beings,
Oh you who were born of Earth,
Oh you who dwell in the sky!

Now the birds that inhabit the air,
Birds from the low world to the great birds,
Birds that float above the clouds.
All these you did think would be a benefit to mankind.
Oh you who were born of Earth,
Oh you who dwell in the sky!
Now we ask that this thought should be forever
Even as long as earth endures.

Now again the smoke arises,
Continue to listen as you inhale this incense,
For we are discussing the things of your creation
That you did think should be a benefit to mankind,
Oh you who were born of Earth,
Oh you who dwell in the sky!
Now you did think that there should be a world and that it should become cold,
At a recurring season become cold again.
Now we implore thee that it should not be too great a cold
And likewise when the earth becomes warm again,
That the heat should be moderate and comfortable.
Now again the smoke arises
To you who were born of Earth,
To you who dwell in the sky!

So now another.
Continue to listen!
You did think that there should be a wind
And that it should be a help to the world.

Now the wind is here.
And the people pray that it may continue to be so as long as earth endures.

Now again the smoke arises
To you who were born of Earth,
To you who dwell in the sky!
Now they came from the west.
Ti′sōt we call them,
Our great grandfathers the Thunderers;
You did make them our relatives.
They were placed in a high position
That they might care for the earth
And feed the waters that flow over the world and purify them,
And freshen all things that grow.
A certain season was appointed for their activity
The season when the earth commences to become warm again.
Now again the smoke arises,
It lifts our words to you,
Oh inhale the incense and continue to listen,
Oh you who were born of Earth,
Oh you who dwell in the sky!
Now the whole world prays that you will listen,
May all these things continue as long as earth endures,
Oh you who were born of Earth,
Oh you who dwell in the sky!

So now again another.
You did think that there should be a sky
And that within it should be something to illuminate the world,
Ēndē′ka gää′′kwa, our great brother, the mighty warrior, the Sun,
And that so it should be called so.
He has a high position that shall last as long as earth endures.
Now again the smoke arises and so smoke tobacco as you listen,
Oh you who were born of Earth,
Oh you who dwell in the sky!
Now the people of all earth with one voice implore you
That your plan may be carried out and continue as long as earth endures,
So do your descendants pray.

So now another.
It is of Soi'kā gää''kwa, our grandmother, the Moon in the sky.
You did make her a sign for reckoning the years of children.
Now she has fulfilled the design of her creation so far.
Now again the smoke arises.
Inhale the incense as you continue to listen,
Oh you who were born of Earth,
Oh you who dwell in the sky!
Through the smoke we pray that this may be so as long as earth endures,
So pray your descendants,
Oh you who were born of Earth,
Oh you who dwell in the sky!
So have they said,
Oh you who were born of Earth,
Oh you who dwell in the sky!

Now you did think that there should be a sky
And that spots should be in the sky
For signs unto the people.
So did you design this to be so as long as the earth endures.
And the people implore thee that this may continue to be as long as the earth endures.
Now again the smoke arises,
And through it the people speak.
Oh inhale as you continue to listen,
Oh you who were born of Earth,
Oh you who dwell in the sky!
Now you did design all that which should occur in the world,
And planned the four sacred ceremonies
That should be perpetuated forever
And celebrated by the people each year.
Be celebrated by these who call themselves your descendants;
That there should be head ones and their assistants
To perpetuate the four ceremonies.
Now as many men-beings as remain on earth are here,
Gathered about this pole.
Now then you have seen that we commenced at the new part of day.
Now you shall know that you are invited to listen to thanking songs this day!

[The head chief yells Yokadi!¦Gowagannie!
The people answer wo' wo' wo'!]

Now tomorrow morning you must consider yourself invited to the Great Feather Dance!

[Cries by the head chief Hioh, hiu, hiu, hiu!
The people answer Io' io' io' io' io'!]

Two parts will be celebrated, the Great Feather Dance and the Harvest Thanksgiving.

[Cries by the head chief, Ganio ganio ganio!
Answers by the the people Ho-ni ho-ni!]

These two ceremonies will be in progress tomorrow,
Oh you who were born of Earth,
Oh you who dwell in the sky
And the next day you are invited to the sacred game.

[Cries by the head chief, Ba-a'! ba-a'! ba-a'! ba-a'! ba-a'!
Answers by the people, Hoie! hoie! hoie! hoie!]

Now again the smoke arises
The incense of the sacred tobacco,
To you who were born of Earth,
Yet dwell in the sky
Only this can we do
To fulfil the law.
All the things of your creation that you have made visible to us
We thank you for and for all the things that you have created.
In the manner that you did think, we have thanked you,
From low earth upward to the great sky where you are living.
With all their strength the people thank you and you have seen it,
Oh you who were born of Earth,
Oh you who dwell in the sky!
So now it is done.
Now you did think that you would appoint four messengers whose work should be to watch over earth
And the people that dwell in the world
To keep them all from harm,
For men-beings are your children.
Now do I say, the voices of the people combine as one
To thank you.
We have done as best we can in giving thanks to the four messengers.
Now again the smoke arises,
And we speak through its incense.
Inhale the smoke as you do listen.
Oh the great Handsome Lake!

We believe that he is happy in the place that you have prepared for him.
Moreover we thank him.
Oh you who were born of Earth,
Oh you who dwell in the sky!
Now only this can we do.
You thought that it should be this way,
Oh you that were born of Earth,
Oh you who dwell in the sky!
Now we thank you, the Creator of the World.
Here are gathered so many people as remain,
Few head men remain.
Only this can we do,
And they say how the people should act.
Of the head men and their cousins only so many are left,
[But they with] the men and the women
The children that run and the children that creep
As one man-being offer you thanks.
They are your descendants,
Oh you who dwell in the sky!
Now you did think that we should offer you tobacco when we addressed you.
And we have fulfilled your request and used tobacco.
We leave our words with you until the next great thanksgiving,
Until then may the people continue in health.
Now the smoke arises!
Oh inhale as you do listen!
Only this can we do
For all the words are spoken
To you, our great ancestor,
Oh you who dwell in the sky.
Oh you who were born of Earth!

NE GANEOWO[1]

One of the four sacred ceremonies of the Seneca

The Gānē′oⁿwoⁿ is a ceremonial thanksgiving in which two "preachers," standing on either side of a long bench around which a company of religious dancers have arranged themselves, alternately intone sections of the Gānē′oⁿwoⁿ ritual. At the end of

---

[1] Ne″gānē′oⁿwoⁿ, recorded and translated at Newtown, Cattaraugus reservation, January 1906.

each section the speaker starts a chant which is taken up by the singers who sit on the benches. A drummer keeps time by beating a water drum and the dancers gracefully circle around the benches. The direction of this dance, as all Iroquois dances, is counterclockwise. When the chant and dance have continued a period deemed sufficient by the opposite speaker, he halts the singing and dancing by the exclamation "Gwi″yă'!" and then commences his intonation.

The writer had recorded the entire Gāně'oⁿwoⁿ ritual, speeches and songs, on a set of phonograph records, especially for preservation by the New York State Education Department. Unfortunately these perished in the Capitol fire of March 29, 1911. About 100 other ceremonial records on wax cylinders were also destroyed at that time.

[PRELIMINARY] TRANSLATION OF THE GANEOWO RITUAL OF THE SENECA

I Gwi″ya'!
Now the whole assemblage is offering thanks!
This day [there] is occurring what the Creator has made pleasing for his own self.
We are thankful that what he has made for himself is accomplished.
[Singing and dancing].

II Gwi″ya'! [Singing and dancing stop].
Now the whole assemblage is offering thanks!
The Creator thought that there should be men-beings,
And he thought that there should be chiefs to regulate the actions of these men-beings.
So now we thank him that what he thought has come to pass!
[Singing and dancing are resumed].

III Gwi″ya'! [Singing and dancing stop].
Now the whole assemblage is offering thanks!
Now he thought that there should be two sexes,
That one should be the female
That children might grow from her.
We thank the women that they are doing their duty in fulfilling the design of their creation.
[Singing and dancing resumed].

IV Gwi″ya'! [Singing and dancing stop].
Now the whole assemblage is offering thanks!
He thought that there should be a difference in the length of lives,
And that children should run about and some creep.
So this is what he has done.
We are thankful that this is fulfilled.
[Singing and dancing resumed].

V Gwi″ya'! [Singing and dancing stop].
Now the whole assemblage is offering thanks!
He thought that certain ones should be the leaders of the people,
The same for both male and female, to preserve the four ceremonies.
So we thank these head ones that they are dutiful to the calling of their Creator.
[Singing and dancing resumed].

VI Gwi″ya'! [Singing and dancing stop].
Now the whole assemblage is offering thanks!
He thought that there should be a world and that people should be upon the world,
That they should draw their sustenance from the world.
So we thank the Creator that what he thought has come to pass.
[Singing and dancing resumed].

VII Gwi″ya'! [Singing and dancing stop].
Now the whole assemblage is offering thanks!
He thought that there should be things in the world for sustenance
And that people should labor for their sustenance.
Now we petition the Creator that we may again see the season of things growing from which our living is.
[Singing and dancing resumed].

VIII Gwi″ya'! [Singing and dancing stop].
Now the whole assemblage is offering thanks!
He thought that there should be herbs of different kinds
And that these should grow when the earth is warm
And that these herbs should be a help to the people when medicine was needed.

So we thank the Creator that what he thought is now occurring.
[Singing and dancing resumed].

IX Gwi″ya'! [Singing and dancing stop].
Now the whole assemblage is offering thanks!
He thought that there should be two different varieties of trees and that one should yield fruit.
Now the first fruit of the year is the strawberry
And he thought that when the strawberries are ripe his creatures should thank him,
Thank him in a great feast and dance ceremony.
Now I ask that the time of strawberries may return again.
[Singing and dancing resumed].

X Gwi″ya'! [Singing and dancing stop].
Now the whole assemblage offers thanks!
He thought that there should be trees for a help to the people of earth.
So now we thank the Creator because what he thought is fulfilled and is a help to the people.
[Singing and dancing resumed].

XI Gwi″ya'! [Singing and dancing stop].
Now the whole assemblage offers thanks!
He thought that there should be a certain tree to bear fruit.
So we are thankful that all things are that he has ordained
And shall be as long as the world endures.
[Singing and dancing resumed].

XII Gwi″ya'! [Singing and dancing stop].
Now the whole assemblage is offering thanks!
He thought that there should be forests upon the earth
That these should be a help to the people of earth.
So we thank the Creator that what he thought has come to pass.
[Singing and dancing resumed].

XIII Gwi″ya'! [Singing and dancing stop].
Now the whole assemblage is offering thanks!
He thought that there should be a certain tree

From which sweet waters should flow when the earth
    warmed.
That this tree should be the maple and that men-beings
    should tap it,
And that this should be a help to the people.
So we thank the Creator that what he thought is occurring.
[Singing and dancing resumed].

XIV Gwi"ya'! [Singing and dancing stop].
Now the entire assemblage is offering thanks!
He thought that there should be a certain tree to yield
    nuts,
So we are thankful that what he thought is so.
[Singing and dancing resumed].

XV Gwi"ya'! [Singing and dancing stop].
Now the whole assemblage is offering thanks!
He thought that he would create wild beasts
And that men-beings should derive benefits from them.
So we thank the Creator that they are [yet] for our help.
[Singing and dancing resumed].

XVI Gwi"ya'! [Singing and dancing stop].
Now the whole assemblage is offering thanks!
He thought that there should be certain ones who should
    be his servants,
And that they should come from the west and care for
    the world,
That they should cause the earth to become wet
Thereby feeding the springs and waters that flow
Moreover that they should be called Hadiwĕnnoda′diĕ‛s,
    the Thunderers.
So we thank the Creator that they have always fulfilled
    the purpose of their creation.
Now we put everything together and say
We are thankful that all things are doing that for which
    they were created.
[Singing and dancing resumed].

XVII Gwi"ya'! [Singing and dancing stop].
Now the whole assemblage is offering thanks!
He thought that there should be a sky over head;
He thought that there should be stars in that sky.

That the men-beings that he put upon the earth might be guided thereby;
That certain stars should guide the people.
So we thank the Creator that what he thought is so.
[Singing and dancing resumed].

XVIII Gwi″ya'! [Singing and dancing stop].
Now the whole assemblage is offering thanks!
Now he thought that there should be a certain one in the sky.
And that he should give light a certain period of time
And that they should call him "our brother, ĕndĕ′-ka gä′äkwa′,"
Now, as we are all gathered together, we thank the sun that he is eternally dutiful.
[Singing and dancing resumed].

XIX Gwi″ya'! [Singing and dancing stop].
Now the whole assemblage is offering thanks!
He thought that there should be another in the heavens
Who should reveal itself when the sun went under
And that people should call it äksŏ″ŏt, our grandmother, Soi′kägä′äkwa.
Now, as we are all gathered together, we thank the moon that she is eternally dutiful.
[Singing and dancing resumed].

XX Gwi″ya'! [Singing and dancing stop].
Now the whole assemblage is offering thanks!
He thought that there must be a certain one who should reveal what he thought.
He thought that he should lay the Gai′wiio′ before the people,
So he revealed the Gai′wiio′ to Ganio′dai′io′
And he did his duty as the Creator had ordained,
He preached and taught until he died.
So we all render our thanks for he has done his duty
For we now follow in the way he taught
And we will remember forever.
[Singing and dancing resumed].

XXI Gwi″ya'! [Singing and dancing stop].
Now the whole assemblage is offering thanks!

He thought that he should have four beings for his messengers
Who should watch over the people of earth and that on their strength their living should be.
Now we thank the four messengers that they are faithful to the design of their creation.
[Singing and dancing resumed].

XXII Gwi″ya'! [Singing and dancing stop].
Now the whole assemblage is offering thanks!
He thought that the people should commence with the lower earth to thank him
For all that he had created and should offer thanks for things from below up to himself in the high world.
We therefore, gathered together in this assemblage, thank our Creator,
Yea all of his creatures who are living in this world.
[Singing and dancing resumed].

XXIII Gwi″ya'! [Singing and dancing stop].
Now all the people offer thanks!
He thought that there should be certain persons to sing for the dances he had made.
Now you who have sung and are singing, we thank you.
[Singing and dancing resumed].
[Speaker exhorts all the people to join in the dance].

OUTLINES OF THE CORNPLANTING AND THE MAPLE THANKSGIVINGS

AN OUTLINE PROGRAM OF WAANO''NAOGWA''CIOT, THE CORNPLANTING CEREMONY

1 Opening address by a chief
2 A Thanksgiving speech
3 Ne''äskä'nīe', the women's dance
4 Ne''ga'dā'ciot, the jubilee dance
5 Ne''gusshědon'dada', the jug shaking dance
6 Ne''äskän'īe', the women's dance
7 Ne''yiĕndoněsshontă', the old women's song
8 Ne''äskä'nīe', the women's dance
9 Ne''gaianon'gayo^{n}ka
10 Ne''ostō'wägo'wa, the great feather dance
11 Closing address
12 Distribution of the feast

The object of the Cornplanting ceremony is to secure divine favor and help in the spring planting. Everyone is invoked to till the ground and earn the bread they eat. The ceremony lasts about four or five hours.

THE MAPLE FESTIVAL

A council is called to set the time for this festival which has no exact day but varies according to the weather. However, it takes place soon after the sap commences to run. Its object is to thank all trees for their services to man and invoke their protection and good will for the coming year.

Outline program

1 The address to the maple tree. A fire is built at the foot of a large maple tree. The people gather around and a special officer advances with a basket of tobacco which he sprinkles on the fire as he recites the address to the maple:

> Ne' něngä' gägwä'ani saiwisa'ane gäni'sĕ swěn'iio'
> Seane ganigä'o ne''niganigai'isek
> One'' dĭq' oyän'kwa(owe)soi'yĕ'
> Negihedahadondi gaiyehonoshäs henizaiwissaho^n'
> One^n'' dĭq' kejedai' soñgwäni, etc.

The prayer at the maple festival
Wa″da Tadinion′nio′o‛
Maple Thanksgiving

Ĕsⁿwaiyĭgwa‛showine″ odēha′donni. Ne″wainnondoi′shoñk
Oh partake of this tobacco the forests.   This we petition
nega′dogä nayŭt′däoⁿ näĕtgonĕ′igais näwä″dä
may you continue the production of sweet water Oh maple
Hawe′oⁿ Nawĕnniio‛ ĕⁿgäoⁿdadegaoⁿ ĕⁿgani′gaiksĕk
The will of the Creator that a certain tree water flows from
Ne″nĕⁿgä′ ĕⁿgä′oñk hadieo″shä deodoⁿoⁿ ne″ hē″hadidŭk′kēnoⁿdiēs
This it   may not accidents   occur   the running about
hadĭksä′shoⁿ′o‛ gahadĕgonⁿshoⁿ
the children   in the woods.

Ne″ neⁿgä″ wănĭshäde‛ ĭs′ ĕsswai′ya‛dagwäni′yothet
Now this   day   you   it belongs to you to enjoy
neⁿgä″ wănĭshä de‛.
this   day.

Djasayawa′godŭk Hawĕn′iio‛ cia″dadē gäoya‛gē′tciojo″.
We give thanks oh God to you the dweller of the heavens.
Agwai′wayiis   ne″gaiyiwanda′kho.
We have done it   what devolved upon us.
Osŭt′gät′ho   djogwŭtgwēnio‛.
You have seen   what we have done.
Da′nē‛ho′.
So, it is.

The address to the maple, the chief of trees and the prayer to the Creator

A Seneca ceremony

The priest stands at the roots of a maple. A fire is burning and the priest casts tobacco in the fire and as its smoke arises he says:

To the tree:

> " O partake of this incense,
> You the forests!
> We implore you
> To continue as before,
> The flowing waters of the maple.

To the Creator and the tree:

> It is the will of the Creator
> That a certain tree
> Should flow such water.
> Now may no accidents occur
> To children roaming in the forests.
> Now this day is yours
> May you enjoy it,— this day.

To the Creator:

> We give thanks, oh God, to you,
> You who dwell in heaven.
> We have done our duty
> You have seen us do it.
> So it is done."

SPECIAL ANNUAL CEREMONIES

I   Dä'nondinônnio'' Ědē'kwa gää'kwa', the Sun Dance.
II   Dä'nondinônnio'' Soi'ka gää'kwa', the Moon Dance.
III Wasaze,[1] the Thunder Dance.

I

1 Dä'nondinônnio'' Ěndē'ka gää'kwa', the Sun dance, is designed to honor the sun.

2 This ceremony has no certain time for its celebration but may be called by anyone, at any time, who dreams it necessary for the welfare of the settlement.

3 The ceremony begins at noon when arrows are shot up toward the sun while the populace shout their war cries.

4 A fire is built outside and tobacco is thrown by a priest who chants the sun-rite.

5 Three times during this ceremony a shower of arrows are shot up to the sun accompanied by a chorus of cries, intended to notify him that they are addressing him.

6 Immediately afterward the Osto'wägowa is engaged in as the only fitting dance to perform before the mighty Sun.

II

1 Dä'nondinônnio'' Soikagää'kwa', the Moon Dance ceremony, is convened by anyone who dreams it necessary or by the advice of a clairvoyant.

---

[1] Meaning, Dakota, or Sioux.

2 A thanksgiving speech is recited by a chief while he burns the tobacco offering to the moon.

3 As the peach stone gambling game is thought especially pleasing to the moon, the company gambles away the evening.

4 The distribution of the feast terminates the ceremony.

III

1 Wasaze, the Thunder Dance, is one designed to please the spirit of Thunder, Hi''noⁿ.

2 A council is called when the first thunder of the year is heard and a time as immediate as possible set for the Wasaze.

3 The dancers assemble without the council house, an opening address is made by a priest or chief and the dance immediately starts.

4 The line of dancers dance into the long house.

5 Hi''noⁿ is supposed to delight in war songs and these are sung to please him.

6 Tobacco is burned and a thanksgiving speech made to Hi''noⁿ, for his services in the past and he is prayed to continue his favors.

LEGEND OF THE COMING OF DEATH[1]

When the world was first made, men-beings did not know that they must die some time. In those days everyone was happy and neither men, women nor children were afraid of anything. They did not think of anything but doing what pleased them. At one time, in those days, a prominent man was found on the grass. He was limp and had no breath. He did not breathe. The men-beings that saw him did not know what had happened. The man was not asleep because he did not awaken. When they placed him on his feet he fell like a tanned skin. He was limp. They tried many days to make him stand but he would not. After a number of days he became offensive.

A female man-being said that the man must be wrapped up and put in the limbs of a tree. So the men did so and after a while the flesh dropped from the bones and some dried on. No one knew what had happened to cause such a thing.

Soon afterward a child was found in the same condition. It had no breath. It could not stand. It was not asleep, so they said. The men-beings thought it was strange that a girl man-being should act this wise. So she was laid in a tree. Now many others did these things and no one knew why. No one thought that he himself would do such a thing.

There was one wise man who thought much about these things and he had a dream. When he slept the Good Minded spirit came to him and spoke. He slept a long time but the other men-beings noticed that he breathed slowly. He breathed [nevertheless]. Now after a time this man rose up and his face was very solemn. He called the people together in a council and addressed the people. The head men all sat around with the people.

The wise man spoke and he said, " The Good Minded spirit made every good thing and prepared the earth for men-beings. Now it appears that strange events have happened. A good word has come to me from the Good Minded spirit. He says that every person must do as you have seen the other persons do. They have died. They do not breathe. It will be the same with all of you. Your minds are strong. The Good Minded spirit made them that way so that you could endure everything that happened. So then do not be downcast when I tell you that you all must die. Listen

---

[1] Related by Edward Cornplanter, March 1906.

further to what I say. The name of the one that steals away your breath is S'hondowĕk'owa. He has no face and does not see any one. You can not see him until he grasps you. He comes sometimes for a visit and sometimes he stays with us until many are dead. Sometimes he takes away the best men and women and passes by the lesser ones. I was not told why he does this thing. He wants to destroy every person. He will continue to work forever. Every one who hears me and every one not yet born will die. There is more about you than living. Any moment you may be snatched by S'hondowĕk'owa, he who works in the thick darkness.

You must now divide yourselves into nine bands, five to sit on one side of the fire and four on the other and these bands shall care for its members. You must seek out all good things and instruct one another, and those who do good things will see when they die the place where the Maker of all things lives."

THE FUNERAL ADDRESS [1]
Awēyondo' Gawen'notgä'o

Now all hearken to what must be said!

We are gathered here because of what our Creator has done. He made it so that people should live only a certain length of time none to be more favored than another.

Now our uncles made provisions for this event, and our grandfathers and the chiefs when they first thought of this thing [death] in those days. They had never seen death [before]. Their first knowledge came when they saw a person in an assembly die. [Strangely] no one was surprised. Soon afterwards they saw another death in the manner of the first. Soon again another died. Then did the chiefs consider the matter, saying, "We were not born to live forever." Then did the people see that they were not to live forever but only for a certain period of time. Therefore, they made certain rules. Then did they divide the people into clans, kashadenioh. Then did they divide the clans into two divisions. Now when a death occurred the other division [phratry] was to officiate at the funeral. The side that lost one of its members must quietly mourn and say nothing. The cousins must do the speaking. They must speak telling the mourners what they must think. So now first they should say, "Keep your minds up."

The preacher then turns to the mourners and addresses them as follows:

There are many of your own relations yet remaining, there are old folk and there are children. So let these lift up your minds. Moreover here is the earth upon which we tread, everything upon it is for our comfort. There is water, springs of water and streams of water flowing over the earth. There are different plants and trees. All of these our Creator has given us. So let this lift up your minds.

So now then another.

There is the sky above our heads. There are many things there. In the forms of the stars are signs to guide us. The sun gives us light. The moon gives us light. She is our grandmother. The sun is our brother. All these are performing that for which they were created. So let this lift up your minds.

So now then another.

---

[1] Related by Skidmore Lay, Cattaraugus chief, March 1900.

It is the Gai'wiio', the good word of our Creator. Our Creator thought that the people should hear what was in his mind. So he sent word down to the earth. He thought that the people should know what his words were. Now this should lift up your minds.

So now then another.

It is the four geniewage [ceremonies]. Now this should lift up your minds.

[If the dead person is a chief the preacher here ceases to give the chief on the mourning side an opportunity to reply. The reply is as follows]:

Cousin! I have heard all that you have laid before us — how we should keep our minds. We have commenced from the beginning of the world when the Creator made us. We have thought of the water, the springs and the streams of water. We have thought of the sky and everything therein, the sun and the moon, the words of our Creator and the four ceremonies. These things you have pointed out, Oh Cousin! These things will lift up our minds. Now, Cousin, you should know that we accept all that you have said. We can not say that we do not accept what you have said. Now we put all of your words together; we accept them all. So is the reply.

[The preacher then arises and continues]:

So now again listen, all of you!

Now let every one listen.

[The preacher makes an extemporaneous speech in which he addresses the entire assembly. Afterward he selects passages from the Gai'wiio' among which the following is always repeated]:

So now another message.

Now it is said that your people must change certain customs. It has been the custom to mourn at each recurring anniversary of the death of a friend or relative. It is said that while you are on earth you do not realize the harm that this works upon the departed.

[Now moreover, it is said that when an infant is born upon the earth with which the parents are dissatisfied it knows and says, " I will return to my home above the earth."]

Now it is said that grief adds to the sorrows of the dead. It is said that it is not possible to grieve always. Ten days shall be the time for mourning and when our friends depart we must lay grief aside. When you, the beings of the earth, lose one of your number you must bury your grief in their grave. Some will die today and some tomorrow, for all our days are numbered. So hereafter do not grieve. Now it is said that when the ten days have elapsed to prepare a feast and the soul of the dead will return and partake of it with you. It is said moreover that you can journey with the dead only as far as the grave. It is said that when you follow a body to the grave you must have prepared for that journey as if to travel afar. Put on your finest clothing for every human creature is on its journey graveward. It is said that the bodies of the dead have intelligence and know what transpires about them. It is true.

So they said and he said. Eniaiehuk. (Section 67 of the Gai'wiio'.)

[The preacher then announces certain decisions of "the dead side" and then continues with the established funeral rite, as follows]:

When the body of the dead is buried we must become resigned to our loss. It can not be helped.

[The preacher speaks to the fathers]:

Now do you also do the same as the dead side and become resigned to your sorrow?

[The preacher addresses the relatives afar off]:

And now you afar off who are the relatives of the dead, do you become resigned also when you hear of the loss?

The things of the past shall continue. It [death] should not hamper or stop any ordination of the Creator. Let not a death stop an event in course of progress. Let us fulfil the law of mourning for a ten-day period and have the feast at the end. We believe that the dead will return at the end of ten days. Now the Creator said, "The customs ordained by the early chiefs [regarding mourning] are right. They had no knowledge of what would happen in the future when they made the customs but the Creator soke to Ganio'dai'io and said, 'True and good is the ceremony of your grandfathers for the time of mourning and also the death feast.'"

[When the face of the dead is unwrapped for its friends to look upon for the last time the preacher says]:

Now let all journey to the grave with the body of the dead for it is as far as we can go.

[At the grave the preacher turns to the crowd and says]:

So now we thank all those who have come to this funeral ceremony to help us. So it is done.

[The body is then covered with earth.]

THE DEATH FEAST [1]

Wainonjää'´koⁿ'

Now let all listen, all ye who are here assembled!

Cousins! We all are familiar with the happening of a few days ago. We are [therefore] here because of what the Creator has done.

Now the relatives have made arrangements. They have promised to obey the commands of the four messengers who said, " It is right to have a feast for the dead. Therefore this thing should be done."

Ten days have passed. Now the relatives of the dead have made preparations and the feast is ready for the dead. Now let this be in your minds, all ye who are here present.

[The preacher here pauses. At his side sits the speaker for the mourners. In his charge is a bundle containing various gifts for those who have aided the bereaved family. The speaker has been told to whom the various presents are to go, and as the preacher pauses and bends down to receive the formal instructions he hands him the first gift. Sitting among the women mourners is a woman, the "mistress of the ceremonies," whose duty is to deliver the gifts to the intended recipients.

After listening to the directions of the speaker the preacher resumes]:

So now the bereaved offer thanks. They thank the one who cared for the body of the dead and dressed it for burial. To that one they give this as a testimony. [The preacher names the article and the matron rising from her seat receives it and delivers it to the person named].

[The preacher again bends to the speaker at his side and receives the " second word." Again facing the audience he proceeds]:

So now of another they have thought. It is of the night watcher [or night watchers]. To this one [or to these ones], they give this roll of cloth [or skins]. And this is your thanks.

[The speaker hands the preacher the roll and he hands it to the matron who delivers it. Stooping and listening to the whispered instructions for the delivery of the next gift, the preacher after making sure that he understands straightens and again speaks]:

---

[1] Related by Edward Cornplanter, March 1906.

Now to him who wrapped the body in its burial covering [or made the coffin], the relatives offer thanks.

[The gift is bestowed as previously described.]

Now the matron who has managed the funeral receives a gift of thanks.

[This named person being the one who has first received and given the gifts now remains seated while the wife or sister of the preacher rises and receiving the gift bestows it. According to Iroquois etiquette it would be an improper thing for the matron to receive her own gift and bear it before the eyes of the crowd to her seat. The recipients are supposed not to be eager to receive the gifts, the things that once belonged to the dead. Besides according to Iroquois philosophy one can not give one's self a thing.]

Now she who notified the people — the relatives desire to give thanks and offer this gift.

Now those who dug the grave — to you the relatives give thanks and offer gifts.

And now you the good friends and relatives, of what is remaining receive you this gift. [The preacher names each person for whom a gift is intended, repeating the formula given. If property of considerable value as live stock or lands is left, the speaker for the mourners in behalf of the council of heirs tells the preacher their decisions and they are announced before the audience. The modern "death feast law" provides that in the event of a man's death his property must go to his children. If he is without issue, then it reverts to his wife. If he was unmarried it was given to the nearest of kin. The law further provides that the property must be divided and apportioned at the "death feast." By the old law the nearest of kin on the clan (maternal) side received the property. Children did not ordinarily inherit their father's property, but their mother's. Their "mother's husband's" belongings went to the kin of the clan to which he belonged.]

[If the dead were an officer of any kind, the preacher announced who was to take his or her place. In order that this election be valid the person chosen must stand, if possible, in the very spot where the dead person expired.]

Now I have finished speaking for the relatives.

Now listen to another matter, all ye who are here present.

Now at this time let the [mourning] relatives cease their grieving. Now may they go and do whatsoever they wish. They are the same as ever and may speak as they please again. Now can they be notified of things to be done. They have now the right to engage in any current happening. No longer think their hands must be held back. If it is possible to do, now do, for the time of mourning has passed.

So now we have done our part for you, cousins. So I have done.

[The preacher resumes his seat.]

[The speaker for the mourning side arises and addresses the officiating side]:

Now listen cousins!

We have heard all that you have said and [know that] you have done your part. We believe that you have done your part. You must hold in your minds that we thank you for what you have done for us. Now I give you this [the object is named] for your trouble.

[Although the speaker is standing at the side of the preacher, the latter can not receive the gift direct, but the matron rising from her seat takes the offering and holds it out to him. Even then he does not take it but points to his wife or mother, indicating that it is to be placed in her keeping.]

[The speaker continues]:

Now we must ask your pardon for giving so small a gift; it is small and your services have been great.

Now we relieve you of your duties, the duties for which we bound you. Now you are relieved.

[The preacher rises and says]:

Now all listen to a few more words that I shall say!

Let all the people here gathered keep silent. Now is the time for the distribution of the feast. It will now be distributed, for it has been prepared and we must eat. Now let they who did the cooking distribute. Let all tarry until the feast is finished. Let hard feelings affect no one and let the matrons divide equally and overlook none. So it is finished.

SECRET MEDICINE SOCIETIES OF THE SENECA[1]

During the last six years the writer has made a detailed field study of the various phases of Iroquois culture, special attention being directed to the rites and ceremonies of the semisecret orders and societies that yet survive among the so-called pagan Iroquois. It was only after diligent inquiry that the actual existence of these societies was clearly established. The False Face Company and the Secret Medicine Society, better termed The Little Water Company, have been known to ethnologists for some time, but no one has adequately described them or has seemed fully aware of their significance. Likewise certain dances, such as the Bird, the Bear, the Buffalo, the Dark, and the Death dances, have been mentioned. Ceremonies also, such as the Otter ceremony and the Woman's song, have been listed, but that back of all these ceremonies there was a society never seems to have occurred to anyone. The Indians do not volunteer information, and when some rite is mentioned they usually call it a dance. Through this subterfuge the existence of these societies has long been concealed, not only from white investigators but from Christian Indians as well, the latter usually professing ignorance of the "pagan practices" of their unprogressive brothers.

Even so close an observer as Lewis H. Morgan says: "The Senecas have lost their Medicine Lodges, which fell out in modern times; but they formerly existed and formed an important part of their religious system. To hold a Medicine Lodge was to observe their highest religious mysteries. They had two such organizations, one for each phratry, which shows still further the natural connection of the phratry and the religious observances. Very little is now known concerning these lodges or their ceremonies. Each was a brotherhood into which new members were admitted by formal initiation."[2]

Morgan's experience is that of most observers, close as their observation may be. The writer, with the assistance of his wife, however, living with the "pagans" and entering fully into their rites, discovered that the "medicine lodges," so far from having become extinct, are still active organizations exercising a great

---

[1] Adapted from the author's article in American Anthropologist, 2:2, April-June, 1909.
[2] Morgan, Ancient Society, p. 97, ed. 1907.

amount of influence not only over the pagans but also over the nominal Christians.

It was found that the organization and rites of the societies might best be studied among the Seneca, who have preserved their rituals with great fidelity. The Onondaga, although keeping up the form of some, have lost many of the ancient features and look to the Seneca for the correct forms.

The teachings of Ganio'dai'io', Handsome Lake, the Seneca prophet, revolutionized the religious life of the Iroquois to a large extent, its greatest immediate effect being on the Seneca and Onondaga. Later it greatly influenced the Canadian Iroquois, excepting perhaps the Mohawk about the St Lawrence. Handsome Lake sought to destroy the ancient folk-ways of the people and to substitute a new system, built of course upon the framework of the old. Finding that he made little headway in his teachings, he sought to destroy the societies and orders that conserved the older religious rites, by proclaiming a revelation from the Creator. The divine decree was a command that all the animal societies hold a final meeting at a certain time, throw tobacco in the ceremonial fires, and dissolve. The heavenly reason for this order, Handsome Lake explained, was that men were acquainted with the effects of their familiarity with the spirits of the animals, which, although they might bring fortune and healing to the members of the animal's order, might work terrible harm to men and to other animals.

The chiefs who were friendly to the prophet and others who were frightened by his threats met in counsel and proclaimed that all the animal and mystery societies should immediately dissolve, and, by their order, were dissolved and disbanded. This they did without holding a hayänt'wŭtgŭs, tobacco-throwing ceremony, as directed. The members of the societies, therefore, declared that the order of the council was illegal and not binding, that the sin of disobedience was upon the chiefs and not upon the body of members. The societies consequently continued their rites, although they found it expedient to do so secretly, for they were branded as witches and wizards,[1] and the members of one society at least were executed as sorcerers when they were found practising their arts.

The existence of the societies became doubly veiled. The zealous proselytes of the New Religion denied their legality and even their existence, and the adherents of the old system did not care to

---

[1] The modern Iroquois call all sorcerers and conjurers, regardless of sex, "witches." They never use the masculine form.

express themselves too strongly in the matter of proclaiming their sacred orders still very much alive. The rites of the societies were performed in secret places for a number of years after the advent of the prophet, but as the adherents of the New Religion became more conservative, the societies again gradually entered into public ceremonies held in the council houses on thanksgiving occasions. At such times some of them gave public exhibitions of their rites; others had no public ceremonies whatsoever. With the gradual acceptance of the New Religion by the great majority of the people, the older religious belief was blended into the new. The Iroquois regard it as their Old Testament. The tabooed societies became bolder in their operations, and the new religionists entered their folds with few if any qualms.

It was about this time that their policy seems to have changed, for after some inquiry the writer can find no restriction placed on membership by reason of phratry or clanship. Candidates might join any society regardless of clan except the society of Men-who-assist-the-women's-ceremonies, which is not a secret organization. This society consists of two divisions, the membership of a division being determined by phratry. It is purely a benevolent society, however, and has nothing to do with "medicine." The various societies of all kinds had, and still have, individual lodges, each of which is nominally independent of any jurisdiction save that of its own officers. The leaders, however, confer and keep their rites uniform. At present, especially in the Little Water Company, it is not even necessary for the song-holder, the chief officer, to be a pagan. This company is the only one which can boast of any great Christian membership or of a lodge composed entirely of nominal Christians. This lodge is the Pleasant Valley Lodge of the Little Water Company on the Cattaraugus reservation. Mrs Harriet Maxwell Converse joined this lodge in 1892, afterward joining the pagan lodge at Newtown.

A careful study of the Iroquois societies will lead to the conclusion that most of the societies are of ancient origin and that their rituals have been transmitted with little change for many years. Indeed, that under the circumstances any changes should have been made would be stranger than that none had occurred at all. Most of the rituals are chanted in unison by the entire company of members, and any change in note, syllable, or word would immediately be detected. Rites transmitted by song are more difficult to change than simple recitals where musical rhythm is not correlated with the word. Some of the rituals, moreover, contain archaic words and expressions, and even entire sentences are not understood by the singers.

Each society has a legend by which its origin and peculiar rites are explained. Most of these legends portray the founder of the society as a lost hunter, an outcast orphan, or a venturesome youth curious to know what was farther on. The founder got into strange complications, saw strange or familiar animals engaged in their rites, was discovered, forgiven, adopted, kept a captive, and finally, after long study and many warnings, was sent back to his people to teach them the secrets of the animals and how their favor could be obtained. The secrets were to be preserved by the society which the hero was to found.[1] There are some variations of this abstract, but it covers the general features of most of the legends.

The study of the societies was commenced by the writer in 1902, and during the years 1905-6 an almost uninterrupted study was made for the New York State Education Department, and the results deposited in the State Library. Since that time the research has been continued for the New York State Museum. Paraphernalia have been collected, phonograph records have been made of many of the songs and ceremonial speeches, texts have been recorded and translated, legends have been gathered, and some music has already been transcribed. There still remains an enormous amount of work to be done, and it is greatly to be regretted that a multiplicity of duties bars the way for as speedy progress in this work as might be desirable, especially since many of the informants are old people and in ill health.

A brief outline of the various societies is presented in this paper. It is impossible for the sake of brevity to present a fair compend or even a systematic outline. The main features of the less known organizations and some neglected facts of the few that are better known are mentioned, it being hoped that even such statements may be useful to students of ethnology. The list follows.[2]

NIGANĔGA″A‘ O.Ä‘ NO′, OR NE″ HONO″TCINO″GÄ. THE LITTLE WATER COMPANY

This society is perhaps the best organized of all the Seneca folk-societies. It holds four meetings each year, but only on three occasions is the night song, Ganoda, chanted. To describe ade-

---
[1] Myths and Legends of the Iroquois, N. Y. State Mus. Bul. 125, p. 176.
[2] A description of some of these societies was prepared for incorporation in the Fifth Annual Report of the Director of the State Museum, 1909.

quately the rites of this society would require a small volume. For the purposes of this paper, since the society has been described at greater length elsewhere, only a few notes can be given.

The company is organized to perform the rites thought necessary to preserve the potency of the "secret medicine," niganĕga"a', known as the "little-water powder." The meetings, moreover, are social gatherings of the members in which they can renew friendship and smoke away mutual wrongs, if any have been committed. It is contrary to the rules to admit members having a quarrel unless they are willing to forgive and forget. Both men and women are members. Its officers, in order of their importance, are: the song-holder, the chief matron, the watcher of the medicine, the feast-makers, invoker, flute-holder, and announcers and sentinels. There are two altars, the Altar of the Fire and the Altar of the Mystery. The ritual consists of three sets of songs describing the various adventures of the founder, known as the Good Hunter. At the close of each section the feast-makers pass bowls of berry juice, giving each singer a draft from a ladle. In some lodges a pipe is passed. An intermission then follows, during which the members, men and women alike, smoke the native home-grown tobacco. The singing is accompanied by the shaking of gourd rattles, and each member shakes one while he sings. Only purified members are supposed to enter. Unclean men or women, even though members, are debarred. The society has no public ceremony and no dances. Only members are supposed to know the precise time and place of meeting. The songs must never be sung outside of the lodge-room, but special meetings are sometimes called for the purpose of instructing novices. The office of song-holder by the Cattaraugus Seneca is hereditary to the name O'dän'kot, Sunshine. The present song-holder of the Ganun'dasē lodge, the pagan lodge at Newtown, Cataraugus reservation, is a youth who is learning the song, George Pierce, the former O'dän'kot, having recently died. Visitors may listen to the songs in an outer room, but are debarred from viewing the "mysteries." Each member, on entering, deposits his medicine packet on the Altar of the Mystery and places his contribution of tobacco in the corn-husk basket. The tobacco is thrown into the fire by the invoker as he chants his prayer to the Creator, the Thunder Spirit, and to the Great Darkness. The flute-song is played during the second and third sections. At the close of the ceremony a pig's head is passed and pieces of the boiled meat are torn from the head with the teeth, the members cawing in imitation of crows. In early times a bear's head was eaten. The food is then distributed, and the meeting or

Fig. 3 The medicine outfit, husk tray, medicine bundle, rattle and flute

" sitting " is concluded. The ceremony commences at about 11 o'clock p. m. and is adjourned at daybreak. The sun " must not see the rites." The business of the society is all conducted before the ceremony commences; reports of the officers are given and the treasurer's report read. The paraphernalia of this society consist of the medicine bundles, the flute, gourd rattles for each singer, the sacred tobacco basket and a bark dipper. The necessary furnishings are a table and a fireplace, these being the " altars," and a lamp. The " medicine " is not used in the ceremonies; it is simply " sung for." Its power is conserved for use by the medicine people in healing ceremonies. The singing of the ritual is conducted in total darkness, the lights being brought in only during the intermissions.

DEWANONDIISSO^NDAIK'TA', PYGMY SOCIETY, THE DARK DANCE CEREMONY

The ritual of this society consists of 102 songs, divided into four sections, as follows: The first section, 15 songs; the second, 23 songs; the third, 30 songs, and the fourth, 34 songs. The order of the ceremony is somewhat like that of the Medicine Company. All the songs are sung in darkness. It is believed that the spirit members of the society come and join in the singing, and their voices are thought to be audible at times.

The water drum and the horn rattle are used in this ceremony for keeping time. There is a brief dance. The Dark ceremony is designed to appease certain spirits and to procure the good offices of others. Meetings are called at any time for the purpose of appeasing the spirits of certain charms that have become impotent or which may become so, or are called by members and even by nonmembers who are troubled by certain signs and sounds, such as the drumming of the water fairies or stone throwers, pygmies, who by their signs signify their desire for a ceremony. Nonmembers become members by asking for the services of the society. The rites are preeminently the religion of the "little folk" whose good will is sought by all Indians living under the influence of the Ongwe'-oñwe'ka', Indian belief. The Pygmies are thought to be "next to the people" in importance, and to be very powerful beings. They demand proper attention or they will inflict punishment upon those who neglect them. This society, however, "sings for" all the "medicine charms" and all the magic animals. These magic animals are members of the society, and in order of their importance are: Joⁿgä'oⁿ, Elves or Pygmies; Jodi"gwadoⁿ, the Great Horned Serpent; Shondowĕk'owa, the Blue Panther, the herald of death; Dewŭtiowa'is, the Exploding Wren. Other members, equal in rank, are: Diatdagwŭt', White Beaver; O'nowaot'gont, or Gane"onttwŭt, the Corn-bug; Otnä'yont, Sharp-legs; O'wai'ta, Little Dry Hand; Dagwŭn'noyaĕnt, Wind Spirit, and Nia"gwahĕ, Great Naked Bear.

These charm-members are called Ho'tcine'gada. The charms or parts of these members, which the human members keep and sing for, are: none of the first two, because they are very sacred and "use their minds" only for charms; panther's claw; feathers; white beaver's castor; corn-bug dried; bone of sharp-legs; dry hand; hair of the wind, and bones of Nia"gwahĕ. Some of these charms bring evil to the owners, but must not be destroyed under any circumstance. Their evil influence can be warded off only by the ceremonies. The owner or his family appoints someone to "hold the charm" after the first owner's death. Other charms are only for benevolent purposes, but become angry if neglected. Of the evil charms, the sharp bone may be mentioned; and of the good charms the exploding bird's feathers. Most of them are regarded, however, as ot'gont. The members of this society save their fingernail parings and throw them over cliffs for the Pygmies.

The ceremonies of the societies are always opened with a speech by the invoker. The following speech is that of the Pygmy Society, and in a general way is the pattern of nearly all opening invocations.

Yotdondak'o', Opening Ceremony of the Pygmy Society

We now commence to thank our Creator.
Now we are thankful that we who have assembled here are well.
We are thankful to the Creator for the world and all that is upon it for our benefit.
We thank the Sun and the Moon.
We thank the Creator that so far tonight we are all well.
Now I announce that A B is to be treated.
Now this one, C D, will throw tobacco in the fire.
Now these will lead the singing, E and F.
So I have said.
[The "tobacco thrower" advances to the fire and, seating himself, takes a basket of Indian tobacco and speaks as follows:]
Now the smoke rises!
Receive you this incense!
You who run in the darkness.
You know that this one has thought of you
And throws this tobacco for you.
Now you are able to cause sickness.
Now, when first you knew that men-beings were on earth, you said,
"They are our grandchildren."
You promised to be one of the forces for men-beings' help,
For thereby you would receive offerings of tobacco.
So now you get tobacco — you, the Pygmies. [Sprinkles tobacco on the fire.]
Now is the time when you have come;
You and the member have assembled here tonight.

Now again you receive tobacco—you, the Pygmies. [Throws tobacco.]
You are the wanderers of the mountains;
You have promised to hear us whenever the drum sounds,
Even as far away as a seven days' journey.
Now all of you receive tobacco. [Throws tobacco.]
You well know the members of this society,
So let this[1] cease.
You are the cause of a person, a member, becoming ill.
Henceforth give good fortune for she (or he) has fulfilled her duty and given you tobacco.
You love tobacco and we remember it:
So also you should remember us
Now the drum receives tobacco,
And the rattle also.
It is our belief that we have said all,
So now we hope that you will help us.
Now these are the words spoken before you all,
You who are gathered here tonight.
So now it is done.

DAWANDO‘, THE SOCIETY OF OTTERS

This is a band of women organized to propitiate the otters and other water animals who are supposed to exercise an influence over the health, fortunes, and destinies of men. The otter, which is the chief of the small water animals, including the fish, is a powerful medicine-animal, and besides having his own special society is a member of the Yě'dos, or I'dos, and the Hono"e-ino"gä‘.

The Otters may appear at any public thanksgiving, as the Green Corn dance and the Midwinter ceremony. After a tobacco-throwing ceremony, hayänt'wŭtgŭs, the three women officers of the Dawan'do‘ each dip a bucket of the medicine-water from the spring or stream, dipping down with the current, and carry it to the council house where they sprinkle everyone they meet by dipping long wisps of corn husk in the water and shaking them at the people. If the women succeed in entering the council house and sprinkling everyone without hindrance, they go for more water and continue until stopped. The only way in which they may be forced to discontinue their sprinkling is for someone, just before she sprinkles him, to snatch the pail and throw the entire contents over her head.

---
[1] The malific influence causing sickness.

The Otter woman will then say, "Hat'gaiï', niawë'!"—meaning, "Enough, I thank you!" She will then retire.

The Otters are especially active during the Midwinter ceremony, and when the water is thrown over their heads it very often freezes, but this is something only to be enjoyed. When possessed with the spirit of the otter, the women are said to be unaware of their actions, and sometimes, when they are particularly zealous, the whistle of the otter is heard. This greatly frightens the people, who regard it as a manifestation of the presence of the "great medicine otter." The women afterward deny having imitated the otter's call, saying that they were possessed of the otter and had no knowledge of what they did.

The Otter Society has no songs and no dances. Its members are organized simply to give thanks to the water animals and to retain their favor. When one is ungrateful to the water animals, as a wasteful fisherman, or a hunter who kills muskrats or beaver without asking permission or offering tobacco to their spirits, he becomes strangely ill, so it is believed. The Otters then go to a spring and conduct a ceremony, after which they enter the sick man's lodge and sprinkle him with spring water, hoping thereby to cure him.

I"DOS OÄ'NO‘, SOCIETY OF MYSTIC ANIMALS

The I"dos Company is a band of "medicine" people whose object is to preserve and perform the rites thought necessary to keep the continued good will of the "medicine" animals. According to the traditions of the company, these animals in ancient times entered into a league with them. The animals taught them the ceremonies necessary to please them, and said that, should these be faithfully performed, they would continue to be of service to mankind. They would cure disease, banish pain, displace the causes of disasters in nature, and overcome ill luck.

Every member of the company has an individual song to sing in the ceremonies, and thus the length of the ceremony depends on the number of the members. When a person enters the I"dos, he is given a gourd rattle and a song. These he must keep with care, not forgetting the song or losing the rattle.

The head singers of the I"dos are two men who chant the dance song. This chant relates the marvels that the medicine man is able to perform, and as they sing he proceeds to do as the song directs. He lifts a red-hot stone from the lodge fire and tosses it like a ball in his naked hands; he demonstrates that he can see through a carved wooden mask having no eyeholes, by finding various things about the lodge; he causes a doll to appear as a living being, and mystifies the company in other ways. It is related that new members sometimes doubt the power of the mystery-man and laugh outright at some of the claims of which he boasts. In such a case he approaches the doll, and though his face be covered by a wooden mask, cuts the string that fastens its skirt. The skirt drops, exposing the legs of the doll. Then the doubting woman laughs, for everyone else is laughing, at the doll she supposes, but shortly she notices that everyone is looking at her, and to her utmost chagrin discovers that her own skirt-string has been cut and that she is covered only by her undergarments. Immediately she stops laughing and never afterward doubts the powers of the medicine-man, who, when he cut the doll's skirt-string by his magic power, cuts hers also.

The I″dos is said to have been introduced among the Seneca by the Huron. The ritual, however, is in Seneca, though some of the words are not understood. The principal ceremonies are: (a) Gai'yowĕⁿ″ogowa, The sharp point; (b) Gahadi′yagoⁿ, At the wood's edge; (c) Gai″doⁿ, The great Gai″doⁿ. Other ceremonies are: O'to'doⁿgwa″, It is blazing; and Tci'gwawa, The other way around. During ceremonies b and c only individual members sing. The chief of the society is said to be a man who is able to see through a wooden mask which has no eye-openings. By his magic power he is able to discover hidden things previously concealed by the members, probably by some particular member. He discovers the ceremonial, no matter where hidden, and juggles with a hot stone drawn from the fire. When the ceremonies are finished the members feast on a pig's head. In early times a deer's head was used. As do the members of the Medicine Lodge upon such an occasion, the members tear the meat from the head with their teeth. The ceremonies of the society are now considered an efficacious treatment for fevers and skin diseases. The rites are supposed to be strictly secret.

The writer has transcribed the entire text of the I″dos ritual in Seneca and has translated it. Three masks are used in the rites — the Conjuror's mask, the Witch mask, and the Dual-spirit's mask. These masks are never used in the rites of the False Face Company, and differ from them in that they have no metal eyes. A flashlight picture of a corner of the I″dos lodge was made by the writer in January 1900, but the session of the lodge was not one of the "regular" ones

SHA'’DOTGE'A, THE EAGLE SOCIETY

The ritual of the Eagle Society consists of ten songs and a dance. The song is called Ganĕ"gwaē oä"no'. Every member participating in the ceremony paints on each cheek a round red spot. No one but members may engage in its ceremonies, even though these be performed publicly. The Eagle Society's ceremony is regarded as most sacred, in this respect next to the Great Feather Dance, O'stowä'gowa. It is believed that the society holds in its songs the most potent charms known. It is said that the dying, especially those afflicted with wasting diseases, and old people, have been completely restored by its ceremonies. This is because the Dew Eagle, to which the society is dedicated, is the reviver of wilting things.[1] The membership is divided into two classes by phratryship. A person may become a member by dreaming such a thing necessary, or by receiving the rites of the society in case of illness. Special costumes are worn in the ceremonies. In the dance the members divide and stand opposite each other according to phratry, the animals opposite the birds. Two dancers from each phratry are chosen, and one singer from each. The dancers assume a squatting posture and imitate the motions of birds. The physical exertion is intense and requires constant interruption. The dancers and singers continue to dance and sing until completely exhausted, unless someone strikes the signal pole and makes a speech. The dancers then retire to their benches until the speech ends, when the singers take up their song and the dance is continued. After his speech, the speaker, who may be any member, presents the dancers for whom he speaks with a gift of money, tobacco, or bread; but the old custom was to give only such things as birds liked for food. The speeches are usually in praise of one's own clan and in derision of the opposite phratry. At the close, the speakers all apologize for their clannish zeal, and say, as if everyone did not known it, that their jibes were intended only as jests. The dancers each hold in their left hands a calumet fan, made by suspending six heron or four eagle feathers parallel and horizontally from a rod or reed. In their right hands they hold small gourd rattles with wooden handles, or small bark rattles made of a folded strip of hickory bark patterned after the larger False-face bark rattles. The signal pole and the striking stick are spirally striped with red paint. After the

---

[1] The Dew Eagle refreshed the scalp of the Good Hunter by plucking a feather from its breast and sprinkling the scalp with dew from the lake in the hollow of its back.

ceremony, when held in a private lodge, the members feast on a pig's head; but this is a modern substitute for a bear's or a deer's head, though crows' heads once were eaten also.

NIA'GWAI'' OÄ''NO', THE BEAR SOCIETY

The ritual of the Bear Society consists of twenty songs and a dance. During the intermissions in the dance, that is, between songs, the participants eat berries from a pan on the dance-bench, or, in winter, eat honey, taking portions of the comb and eating it as they walk about the bench. The ceremony is opened by making a tobacco offering to the spirits of the bears, during which the chief Bear-man makes an invocation. The high officer of the society, however, is a woman. The symbol of membership is a black streak drawn diagonally across the right cheek. The object of the society is to cure the diseases of its members and candidates by chanting and dancing. The ceremony is believed to be a remedy for fevers and rheumatism, as well as to bring good fortune. In a healing ceremony the chief woman blows on the head of the patient. After a ceremony the members carry home with them pails of bear pudding, a sweetened corn pudding mixed with sunflower oil. The Bears use the water drum and horn rattles. All Seneca dances are counterclockwise.

Fig. 4 Horn Rattle used in the Seneca Bear Dance

DEGI'YA'GOⁿ OÄ''NO', THE BUFFALO SOCIETY

The ritual of this society consists of a number of songs which relate the story of the origin of the order. After a ceremony in which there is a dance, the members depart, carrying with them the buffalo pudding. The dancers imitate the action of buffalo when stamping off flies, and the pudding is supposed to be of the consistency of the mud in which the buffalo stamps. When it is eaten it acts as a charm that "stamps off" disease or ill fortune. The Buffalos use the water drum and horn rattles.

O'GI'WĒ OÄ'NO', CHANTERS FOR THE DEAD

The O'gi'wē ceremony is called for by any member who dreams of the restless spirit of some former member, relative, or friend. At the ceremony the set of songs is sung, the large water drum beaten, and a feast indulged in. The food is supposed to satisfy the hungry ghosts that for some reason are " earth-bound," as spiritists might express it. The O'gi'wē ceremony must not be confused with the Death Feast ceremony, which is a clan affair. The diviner of the O'gi'wē people is able to identify the unknown spirit which may be troubling the dreams of a member. The sickness and ill fortune caused by evil ghosts may be dispelled by the ceremony. The chief officer is a woman.

DESWADENYATIONDOTTŬ', THE WOMAN'S SOCIETY

This society preserves the ritual by which good fortune and health are obtained for women. The singers, fourteen in number at Cattaraugus, are all men. During their singing the women dance. The office of chief singer is hereditary. The women join in a chorus as the men sing. Horn rattles and water drums are used.

TOWII'SAS, SISTERS OF THE DIO'HĒ'KO

This society is composed of a body of women whose special duty is to offer thanks to the spirits of the corn, the beans, and the squashes, Dio'hē'ko (these sustain our lives). By their ceremonies of thanksgiving the Towii'sas propitiate the spirits of growth, and people are assured of a good harvest. The Towii'sas have a ceremonial song and a march, but no dances. The legend of the society relates that the entire band of Towii'sas, in the latter part of the seventeenth century, was captured by the Cherokee and carried down the Ohio river. Thereafter two men were admitted as escorts in their march through the woods. At the closing of the ceremony the head-woman chants the Dio'hē'ko song as she leads her band about a kettle of corn pudding. She carries an armful of corn on the cob; in her right hand she holds some loose beans, and in her left some squash seeds, the emblems of fertility. The Towii'sas hold one ceremony each year, unless some calamity threatens the harvest. The rattle of this society is made of a land tortoise (box-turtle) shell. These are often found in graves, but their exact use in the Iroquois territory has not generally been known to archeologists. The leg rattle is another variety having several perforations.

HADIGOⁿ'SA SHOⁿO', THE FALSE FACE COMPANY

This organization is one of the better known societies of the Iroquois, and its rites have often been described, though not always correctly interpreted. There are three divisions of the False Faces, and four classes of masks — doorkeeper or doctor masks, dancing masks, beggar masks, and secret masks. The beggar and thief masks form no part of the paraphernalia of the true society, and the secret masks are never used in public ceremonies in the council house at the midwinter ceremony. The False Face ceremonies have been well described, though by no means exhaustively, by Morgan[1] and Boyle.[2] The main features are generally known.

The paraphernalia of this society consist of the masks previously mentioned, turtle-shell rattles (snapping turtles only), hickory bark rattles, head throws, a leader's pole upon which is fastened a small husk face, a small wooden false face, and a small turtle rattle, and a tobacco basket.

There are two Seneca legends setting forth the origin of the False Faces, and three with the Mohawk story. These stories, however, explain the origin of different classes of masks. Each mask has a name. One story relates that the False Faces originated with the Stone Gaints. However this may be, the writer obtained in 1905, from a woman claiming to be the keeper of the secret masks, a mask representing the Stone Gaint's face. With it was a mask made of wood, over which was stretched a rabbit skin stained with blood. This mask was supposed to represent the face of a traitor as he would look when drowned for his infamy. Chief Delos Kettle said it was used to cure veneral diseases.

Fig. 5 Typical medicine mask

There is some dispute as to the antiquity of the False Face Company. Doctor Beauchamp, in his History of the Iroquois,[3] says it is comparatively recent. From a study of the Seneca society, however, the writer is inclined to believe that it is quite old with them,

---

[1] Morgan, Fifth Annual Report New York State Cabinet (Museum), 1852, p. 98.

[2] Boyle, Archaeological Report, Provincial Museum, Toronto, 1898, p. 157.

[3] N. Y. State Mus. Bul. 78, p. 141.

although it may be more recent with the other Iroquois. Early explorers certainly could not have seen everything of Iroquois culture, especially some of the secret things, and their lack of description may be regarded as negative testimony rather than as positive evidence of the nonexistence of certain features which later students have found. It is quite possible that the author of " Van Curler's " Journal of 1634-35 mentions a false face when he writes: " This chief showed me his idol; it was a head with the teeth sticking out; it was dressed in red cloth. Others have a snake, a turtle, a swan, a crane, a pigeon for their idols. . . ." The Seneca at present drape their false faces when they hang them up for safe keeping, and use them as well as turtle and snake charms as bringers of good fortune. Some pipes from seventeenth-century graves seem to represent blowing masks. Mr M. R. Harrington and the writer found one in 1903 while excavating a seventeenth-century site, since learned to be of Seneca occupancy, on Cattaraugus creek, near Irving. The counterpart of this pipe was found by R. M. Peck on the Warren site, near West Bloomfield, N. Y. The Indians say it is a False Face blowing ashes, and such it may represent. Mr Harrington, and the writer as well, have found what may be false face eye-disks, as well as turtle-shell rattles, in Seneca and Erie graves.

The principal False Face ceremonies are: Ganoi''iowi, Marching Song; Hodigosshos'ga, Doctors' Dance, and Yeaⁿsĕⁿdădi'yas, Doorkeepers' Dance.

THE OPENING OR TOBACCO THROWING CEREMONY OF THE FALSE FACE COMPANY

Now receive you this tobacco, you, Shagodiowĕⁿ'gowa, the great false face.

Now it is that you have come to where your grandchildren are gathered.

Now you are taking the place of the great false faces who are wandering in the rocky valleys and mountains.

Now you are the ones who think much of this sacred tobacco.

Now we wish to make a request of you. So we always offer this sacred tobacco [literally, real tobacco], when we ask anything of you.

We pray that you help us with your power.

You can go over all the earth.

In the center of the earth is a great pine tree and that is the place of your resting. It is there that you rub your rattle when you come to rest.

Now then this tree receives this tobacco.

We ask that you watch over us and exercise your power to protect us from anything harmful.

We hold in mind that you have ever done your duty in past times and we ask that you continue [vigilant] henceforth.

We use this tobacco when we ask favors of you for you are very fond of this tobacco.

Now your cane gets tobacco. The great pine tree to its top is your cane.

Now you, the husk faces, you get tobacco also.

You have been associated with the false faces in times past. Now you receive tobacco for you have done your duty.

So it is finished.

GAJI'SASHO͞Ⓒ, THE HUSK-FACES

This society seems rather loosely organized among the Seneca, but its chief members act as water doctors. They endeavor to cure certain diseases by spraying and sprinkling water on the patients. Two Husk-faces are admitted with the False Faces in their midwinter long-house ceremony, and act as door-openers. As a company they also have a ceremony in which the Grandfather's Dance is featured. The grandfather is attired in rags, and, holding a cane stationary, dances in a circle about it, using the cane as a pivot. The company dance is one in which all the members participate. Non-members may partake of the medicine influence of the ceremony by joining in the dance at the end of the line when the ceremony is performed in the council house at the midwinter festival.

That the foregoing so-called societies are in fact organizations, and that their rites are not merely open ceremonies in which anyone may engage, is apparent from the following considerations:

1 The organizations have permanent officers for the various parts of their rites.

2 They have executive officers.

3 They have certain objects and stand for specific purposes.

4 They have stable and unchangeable rituals.

5 Those who have not undergone some form of an initiatory rite are not allowed to enter into their ceremonies.

6 They have legends by which the origin and objects of the rites are explained.

7 It is not permissible to recite the rituals or to chant any of the songs outside of the lodge to anyone who has not been inducted into the society.

Some of the societies have other features, such as stated meetings and officers' reports, but the foregoing characteristics apply to all the Seneca secret or semisecret ceremonies and entitle them to the name of *societies*.

When an Indian is afflicted with some disorder which can not be identified by the native herb doctors, the relatives of the patient consult a clairvoyant, who names the ceremony, one of those above described, believed to be efficacious in treating the ailment. Sometimes several ceremonies are necessary, and as a final resort a witch-doctor is called upon.

As to the influence of these organizations on the people, while it must be confessed that they foster some " superstitions " inconsistent with the modern folk-ways of civilized society, they serve more than any other means to conserve the national life of the people. The strongest body of Iroquois in New York today are the two bands or divisions of the Seneca, and the Seneca have the largest number of " pagans." They are perhaps likewise the most patriotic, and struggle with greater energy to retain their tribal organization and national identity.

The customs of these adherents of the old Iroquois religion react on and influence the entire body of the people, " pagans " and Christians alike.

Plate 16

The women's dance

The Seneca buffalo dance

From a drawing by Jesse Cornplanter

The death chant and march at the Newtown Long House

From a drawing by Jesse Cornplanter

Plate 19

The Spirit of the Hurricane

From a drawing by Jesse Cornplanter

Sacrifice of the White Dog on the Grand River reservation of the Six Nations, Canada

Plate 21

A corner of the I'dos lodge at Newtown, Cattaraugus reservation

Ceremonial march of the Toñ'wisas Company. The leader carries an armful of ears of corn in one arm and a tortoise shell in the right hand. From a drawing by Jesse Cornplanter (Gayundaiyeoh, a Seneca boy)

PURIFICATION CEREMONY
of the
Society of Otters

Drawn by
J Complanter

Purification ceremony of the Society of Otters, a Seneca women's winter ceremony

IROQUOIS SUN MYTHS[1]

The Iroquois of New York and Canada still retain vestiges of their former adoration of the sun, and observe certain rites, very likely survivals of more elaborate sun ceremonies.

The writer has witnessed several so-called " sun dances " among the Iroquois; but in every case the dance was the Ostowä"gowa, or Great Feather Dance, the prime religious dance of the Gai'wiio' religion. This modern religion was originated about 1800 by Ganio'dai'io' (" Handsome Lake " the Seneca prophet) and almost entirely revolutionized the religious system of the Iroquois of New York and Ontario. Few of the early folk beliefs have survived the taboo of the prophet; and these beliefs are not easily traced, or even discovered, unless one has before him the Gai'wiio' of Handsome Lake and the Code of Dekanowi'da, the founder of the Confederacy.

The Seneca sun ceremony, Ëndéka Dä'kwa Dännon'dinon'nio' (" Day Orb-of-light Thanksgiving "), is called by any individual who dreams that the rite is necessary for the welfare of the community. The ceremony begins promptly at high noon, when three showers of arrows or volleys from muskets are shot heavenward to notify the sun of the intention to address him. After each of the volleys the populace shout their war cries, " for the sun loves war." A ceremonial fire is built — anciently by the use of a pump-drill, modernly by a match — and the sun-priest chants his thanksgiving song, casting from a husk basket handfuls of native tobacco upon the flames as he sings. This ceremony takes place outside the long house, where the rising smoke may lift the words of the speaker to the sun. Immediately after this, the entire assemblage enters the long house, where the costumed Feather dancers start the Ostowä"gowa.

Among the Onondaga of the Grand River reserve in Ontario, the leader of the sun ceremony carries an effigy of the sun. This is a disk of wood ten inches in diameter, fastened to a handle perhaps a foot long. The disk is painted red in the center, and has a border of yellow. Around the edge are stuck yellow-tipped down-feathers from some large bird. The New York Iroquois have no such effigies, and the writer seriously doubts that the preachers of Handsome Lake's Gai'wiio' would permit such a practice, it being a viola-

---

[1] A. C. Parker in the Journal of American Folk Lore, October–December 1910.

tion of the prophet's teaching. The Canadian Iroquois, however, received the revelations later than their New York brethren, and were longer under the influence of the older religion, which may account for the survival and use of the sun-disk.

The writer has discovered several sun myths among the Seneca, the one which follows being related by Edward Cornplanter, Soson'dowa (" Great Night "), the recognized head preacher of the Gai'wiio' of Handsome Lake. Cornplanter is a Seneca, and a descendant of Gaiänt'waka, the prophet's brother.

The fragments of the cosmological myths which conclude this article are from a mass of ethnological and folk-lore data which it is hoped will shortly be edited and published.

THREE BROTHERS WHO FOLLOWED THE SUN UNDER THE SKY'S RIM

This happened in old times, when there were not many people. There were three brothers and they were not married. They were hunters and had spent their lives hunting. When the brothers were young they enjoyed the excitement of hunting; but as they grew older it did not give them so much pleasure. The youngest brother suggested that for new experiences they walk to the edge of the earth, where the sky comes down and touches the big sea of salt water. There is salt water west, and this world is an island. The other brothers thought the plan a good one; and when they had prepared everything they started on the journey. They traveled a good many years and a good many things happened to them. They always went straight westward.

At last the brothers came to a place where the sun goes under the sky's edge. The sky bends down there and sinks into the water. They camped there for a month and watched the things that happened there. They noticed how the sun got under the rim of the sky and went away quickly. Some men came there and tried to get under the edge of the sky, but it descended quickly and crushed them. There is a road there. Now they noticed that when the sky came up, the water sank lower; and that when the sky went in the water, the water rose higher.

The younger brothers desired to pass under the rim of the sky when the sun slipped under on his road; but the elder brother said that the happenings were too evilly mysterious, and that he was afraid. The younger brothers ran under the rim of the sky quickly, and the rim was very thick. They kept on the road, and water was on each side. They were afraid that the sky would come down and crush them. Now, the oldest brother, it is said, watched them; and when he saw that nothing happened to injure his brothers, he began to run after them. The younger brothers turned from their safe place to encourage him; but the sky came down on the sun's road and crushed him, but they saw his spirit (notwai'shä^n) shoot by quickly. The brothers felt sad.

On the other side of the sky everything is different, so it is said. Before the brothers was a large hill; and when they had ascended it, they saw a very large village in the distance. A man came running toward them. He was in the distance; but he came nearer, and he called out, "Come!" It was their elder brother. "How did you come so quickly, brother?" they asked. "We did not see you come."

The brother answered only, "I was late." He passed by on a road.

An old man came walking toward them. He was youthful and his body was strong, but his hair was long and white. He was an old man. His face was wise-looking, and he seemed a chief.

"I am the father of the people in the Above-the-Sky-Place," he said. "Hawĕni'io' is my son. I wish to advise you because I have lived here a long time. I have always lived here, but Hawĕni'io' was born of the woman on the island. When you see Hawĕni'io', call quickly, 'Niawĕ^n'skäno^n'!' If you fail to speak first, he will say, 'You are mine,' and you will be spirits, as your brother is."

The brothers proceeded and saw a high house made of white bark. They walked up the path to the door. A tall man stepped out quickly, and the brothers said, "Niawĕ^n'skäno^n'!" and the great man said, "Dogĕ^{n}s', I have been watching you for a long time." The brothers entered the house. Now, when they were in the house, the man said, "In what condition are your bodies?" The brothers answered, "They are fine bodies." The great man answered, "You do not speak the truth. I am Hawĕni'io', and I know all about your bodies. One of you must lie down, and I will purify him, and then the other."

One brother lay down, and Hawĕni'io' placed a small shell to his lips, and put it on the brother's mouth. He also tapped him on the neck, and sealed the shell with clay. He began to skin the brother. He took apart the muscles, and then scraped the bones. He took out the organs and washed them. Then Hawĕni'io' built the man again. He loosened the clay and rubbed his neck. He did this with both brothers; and they sat up, and said, "It seems as if we had slept." Hawĕni'io' said, "Every power of your bodies is renewed. I will test you."

The brothers followed Hawĕni'io' to a fine grove of trees surrounded by a thick hedge. All kinds of flowers were blooming outside. "My deer are here," said Hawĕni'io'.

A large buck with wide antlers ran toward them. "He is the swiftest of my runners. Try and catch him," said Hawĕni'io'.

The men ran after the deer, and rapidly overtook him. "He has given us good speed," the brothers said. They soon discovered that they had many surpassing abilities, and the great man tested them all on that day.

They returned to the white lodge, and the brothers saw a messenger running toward them. Upon his wide chest was a bright ball of light. It was very brilliant. In some unknown language he shouted to Hawĕni'io' and dashed on.

"Do you understand his words, or do you know that man?" asked Hawĕni'io'. "He is the sun, my messenger. Each day he brings me news. Nothing from east to west escapes his eye. He has just told me of a great war raging between your people and another nation. Let us look down on the earth and see what is happening."

They all went to a high hill in the middle of the country, and looked down through a hole where a tree had been uprooted. They saw two struggling bands of people and all the houses burning. They could hear people crying and yelling their war cries.

"Men will always do this," said Hawĕni'io', and then they went down the hill.

The brothers stayed a long time in the upper world, and learned so much that they never could tell it all. Sometimes they looked down on the earth and saw villages in which no one lived. They knew that they were waiting for people to be born and live there. In the upper world they saw villages, likewise, awaiting the coming of people. Hawĕni'io' told them a good many things, and after a time told a messenger to lead them to the path that the sun took when he came out on the earth in the morning. They followed the messenger and came out on the earth. They waited until the sun went over the earth and had gone to the west. Again then they went under the edge of the sky in the east, and came out in their country again. It was night, and they slept on the ground. In the morning they saw their own village, and it was overgrown with trees. They followed a path through the woods and came upon another village. Their own people were there, and they went into a council house and talked. They told their story; and no one knew them except their own sister, who was an aged woman.

"The war of which you speak took place fifty years ago," the sister said.

The brothers did not care for the earth now, but wished themselves back in the upper world. They were not like other men, for they never grew tired. They were very strong and could chase animals and kill them with their hands. Nothing could kill them, neither arrows nor disease. After a while, both were struck by lightning, and then they were both killed.

It seems quite likely that there are modern features in this legend; but my informant assured me that the portion relating to the sky and the sun was very old. He said also that he had always heard the upper world described as related in the legend. He added that the sun loved the sound of war, and would linger in his morning journey to see a battle, but that after he reached midheaven he traveled at his usual speed.

Mrs Asher Wright, who spoke Seneca perfectly, and who labored as a missionary among them for fifty years, recorded two Seneca myths as they had been related to her by Esquire Johnson, an old Seneca chief. One describes the origin of good and evil, and says that the sun was made by the Good-minded spirit from the face of his mother. That legend makes the first woman the mother of the twins. The second manuscript, dated 1876, relates practically the same story, but mentions the Sky-woman as having borne first a daughter, who became, without any knowledge of man, the mother of the twins. The mother, having died at their birth, was buried by her mother. The Sky-woman, the grandmother, then turned and addressed the Good-minded spirit, according to Esquire Johnson, quoted by Mrs Wright, as follows:

"Now you must go and seek your father. When you see him, you must ask him to give you power." Pointing to the east, she said, "He lives in that direction. You must keep on until you reach the limits of the Island, and then upon the waters until you reach a high mountain which rises up out of the water, and which you must climb to the summit. There you will see a wonderful being sitting on the highest peak. You must say, 'I am your son.'"

The "wonderful being" appears from the succeeding text to be the sun, although not specifically so named.

We thus have three conflicting ideas presented — the sun as the messenger of the Creator and as the patron of war, as the face of the first mother, and as the father of mankind of earthly origin, although this latter conclusion may be disputed by some for lack of a definite reference.

This leads us to the fact that Iroquois mythology in its present state has been derived from several sources. This has been caused, without doubt, by the policy of adopting the remnants of conquered tribes. Thus we may expect that in Iroquois mythology are the survivals of early Huron, Neutral, Erie, and Andaste elements. It is now possible to trace only the Huron. Algonquian elements came in through the Delaware, the Chippewa, the Shawnee, the Munsee, the Mahikan, and possibly the Nanticoke. It is not difficult to trace Siouan influence.

The writer has been able to trace some of the influencing elements to their sources, but it is nevertheless admitted that the problem of critically sifting and comparing Iroquois myths is a delicate task.

ANECDOTES OF CORNPLANTER
Related by Emily Tallchief, his great great granddaughter

CORNPLANTER MAKES PEACE

"Now these stories are true and came to Solomon Obail from Cornplanter, and Solomon, my father, told me.

"The Cornplanter reservation Senecas often traveled by canoes down the Allegany river to Pittsburgh. On a certain occasion Cornplanter went with a party of canoeists down the Allegany to Pittsburgh. While on his journey one of the paddlers sang Woine'owi as he paddled. Now as he sang the party was startled by a voice that called from the cliff above, 'Halt ye!' The paddler grounded the canoe and Cornplanter went ashore, where, ascending the cliff, he found a number of Indians gathered about a tree to which a white man was bound. 'So now Cornplanter,' said the chief of the band, 'I have called you to kill this man. You may now do as you please with him and we will be satisfied.' Cornplanter drew forth his long hunting knife and feeling of its sharp edge said 'So I may do as I wish. Truly then I shall do so.' So saying he rushed toward the man with upraised knife and brought it down with a flourish. The man was not injured but instead stepped out from the tree free, for Cornplanter's knife had severed the thongs. 'Now,' said Cornplanter, after some conversation with the man, 'I will hire a guide to take this man back to his home in Philadelphia.' A warrior accepted the commission and guided the prisoner safely back to his home where he found him to be a man of prominence, a chief among his people."

"So I say this," added Mrs Tallchief, "to show that my grandfather was a good man, just and kind. Because of these qualities he became influential."

CORNPLANTER AND WASHINGTON

"Now during the war of the thirteen fires against the king of Great Britain, we, the Iroquois, were loyal to our old allies, the British. We fought for them, but, alas for us they were beaten. Now Washington, the great leader of the thirteen fires, was determined to punish us for our part in the war, for he did not realize that we were but keeping our treaties with the British when we fought. So Washington said, 'Depart from among us and go to the west far from the white people.' But Cornplanter said, 'Not so. We are determined not to move. We have long lived here and intend to continue in our own territory as long as we are able to hold it.' 'Not so,' answered Washington, 'you fought against us and therefore you must move on to the west and if you refuse we shall compel you.' 'Then,' answered Cornplanter, 'we will resist you by force of arms. If you win we will have to go, otherwise we will remain where we now are.'

"Cornplanter returned from Washington to his people and spread the news. Quickly it traveled among all the Indians to the south, the east and the west. All were very angry and said, 'We will fight. When the white man tries to move us as they please it is time that we moved a few white men.' Then the western Indians began to massacre the settlers. The news came to Washington. 'It is a mistake to encourage another Indian war,' he said and then sent for Cornplanter. 'I want to settle our difficulties,' said he, 'and I wish peace. I do not wish war, therefore you, Cornplanter, must pacify your people.' 'I care not to meddle further with matters,' said Cornplanter. 'But you must go,' insisted Washington, 'you are the only man who can restore peace and good will.' Thus it was that Cornplanter accepted the commission. He returned home and collecting a party of chiefs sent abroad declarations of peace. The delegation went through Sandusky into the farther west. There Cornplanter called a council and said, 'We must be peaceful with the white men and cease tormenting them.' Now the tribe was a very fierce one and was very angry that Cornplanter advised peace. They mixed poison with the food which they served the delegation and a number died. Cornplanter also was made severely ill. Then Cornplanter became very angry and calling a council said, 'You have acted with treachery. Now I cease to plead. I now command that you let the white people live in peace. Do not kill another one. If you do I will bring the whole Five Nations against you and with a great army of white men will kill every one of you. The Senecas are the greatest nation of all nations and whatever they plan they do. We are always successful and always victorious in sport, debate or battle. So beware.' Now the western Indians councilled among themselves and said, 'We must hastily agree for if the Senecas come against us we surely will be defeated.'"

ORIGIN OF THE NAME CORNPLANTER

"Gaiänt'wakë', the great chief, once went to Philadelphia.

"'How do your people procure food?' asked a white man, a Quaker.

"'We are hunters,' answered the chief.

"'Have you not observed our great fields of corn and grain?' asked the white man, 'and did you know that we never have famines as you do? Why do your people not cultivate gardens of size and till large fields of grain?'

"'My people used to do so,' said the chief, 'and not many years ago when they dwelt in the valley of the Genesee. Now I think that I will encourage this practice again.'

"This conversation so impressed the chief that when he returned he spoke of the matter before the councils and exhorted people in private to plant more and hunt less. Because of this he received the name of *The Planter,* but the whites called him Cornplanter."

KEY TO PHONIC SYSTEM

a   as in *father, bar;* Germ. *haben*
ā   the same sound prolonged
ă   as in *what;* Germ. *man*
ä   as in *hat, man, ran*
ai   as in *aisle,* as i in *mine, bind;* Germ. *Hain*
au as ou in *out,* as ow in *how;* Germ. *Haus*
c   as sh in *shall;* Germ. sch in *schellen;* cio-sho as in *show*
d   pronounced with the tip of the tongue touching the upper teeth
e   as e in *they,* as a in *may;* Fr. *ne*
ĕ   as in *met, get, then;* Germ. *denn;* Fr. *sienne*
g   as in *gig;* Germ. *geben;* Fr. *gout*
h   as in *has, he;* Germ. *haben*
i   as in *pique, machine;* ie as ye in English *yea*
ī   the same sound prolonged io as yo in *you*
ĭ   as in *pick, pit*
j   as in *judge*
k   as in *kick, kin*
n   as in *no, nun, not*
ñ   as ng in *ring, sing*
o   as in *note, boat*
q   as ch in Germ. *ich*
s   as in *see, sat*
t   pronounced with the tip of the tongue on the upper teeth
u   as in *rule;* Germ. *du;* Fr. ou in *doux*
ŭ   as in *rut, shut*
w   as in *wit, win*
y   as in *yes, yet*
dj   as j in *judge*
tc   as ch in *church;* tci-chee as in *cheese*
ⁿ   marks nasalized vowels as aⁿ, eⁿ, ĕⁿ, oⁿ, ăⁿ, aiⁿ, etc.
‘   indicates an aspiration or soft emission of the breadth which is initial or final, thus ‘h, ĕⁿ‘, o‘, etc.
’   marks a sudden closure of the glottis preceding or following a sound, thus ’a, o’, ä’, ă’, etc.
′   marks the accented syllable of a word
t and *h* in this system are always pronounced separately

GLOSSARY OF SENECA WORDS

(For key to pronunciation see page 139)

Adanidä'oshä — (cooperative labor), 39
Adekwe'oⁿge — (green corn thanksgiving), 43
Adĭstowä'ẹ — (feather wearing; name applied to conservative Indians by the more radical), 14
Adoⁿdär'ho — (meaning snaky headed), 5
Adoⁿ'wĕⁿ — (thanking or cheer songs), 41; figure, 84
Askä'nīe' — (women's dance), 101
Awĕ'yondo' gawen'notgä'o — (the funeral address), 107
Dagwŭn'noyaĕnt — (the wind spirit), 119
Daitdagwŭt' — (white beaver), 119
Dänondinōñ'yo — (Thanksgiving), 103
Dawan'do' — (other ceremony), 121
Degi'ya'goⁿ oä"no' — (Buffalo Society), 125
Dewŭtiowa'is — (exploding wren), 119
Diogē"djaie — (grassy place), 75
Diohe"koⁿ — (the corn, bean and squash triad; the word means, They sustain us), 39, 54, 86
Diondēgă' — (Seneca name of Pittsburgh)
Dion'dot — (tree), 75
Dionĭ'hogä'wĕ — (Open Door, or Door Keeper, name of Seneca war sachem, once held by Gen. Ely S. Parker), 12
Diono'sade'gĭ — (place of burnt houses; the Seneca name for Cornplanter village), 20, 52
Djĭs'gäⁿdä'taha' — (ghost talker), 68
Dogĕⁿs' — (truly a reply), 113
Ĕndē'ka gää"kwa — (daytime brilliant orb, the sun), 91
Enīa'iehŭk — (it was once that way; the closing word of each section of the Gai' wiio')
Gadä'ciot — (the trotting dance), 82, 101
Gadägĕs'käoⁿ — (fetid banks), Cattaraugus
Gagwē'goⁿ — (all, everyone, entirely), 33
Gahadi yago — (at the wood's edge, a ceremony), 123
Gaiänt'wakă — (The Planter, commonly called Cornplanter. A Seneca pine tree chief name. The half brother of Handsome Lake), 23, 24, 44, 50

Gai"do[n]	(an I"dos ceremony), 123
Gai'yowĕ[n]'ogowă	(the sharp point; a ceremony), 123
Gai'wiio'	(meaning the good message; pronounced as if spelled guy-we-you), 5, 6, 26, 43
Gai'wiios'tŭk	(the Christian religion), 57
Gaji"sasho[n]o'	(husk false face), 129
Gaknowe'haat	(to copulate), 73
Găko'go'	(she is a gluttonous beast, a name), 74
Ganăwĕ[n]'gowa	(great bowl game), 41
Gănă'yasta'	(midwinter ceremony), 81
Ganĕ"gwaē	(the Eagle dance song), 124
Gane'o[n]wo[n]	(the harvest thanksgiving ceremony), 21, 26, 41, 94
Ganio'dai'io	(Handsome or Beautiful Lake, the title of the sachem name held by the prophet), 5, 18, 22, 46, 80
Ganōda	(night song), 116
Gănonjoni'yon	(Kittle Hangs, a name), 74
Ganonktiyuk'gegăo	(name of Onondaga), 76
Ganos'ge'	(house of the tormentor), 56
Găno[n]'wagĕs	(fetid water, Seneca name for their village near present site of Avon, Livingston co., N. Y.), 9, 78
Ganowoñ'go[n]	(in the rapids, name of Warren, Pa.), 20
Ganŭn'dasē'	(Ga-nun-da-se, meaning *a town new* or Newtown. Name of non-Christian Seneca village on Cattaraugus reservation)
Ganŭndase"ge'	(place of a new town; Seneca name of Geneva), 79
Ganuñg'sĭsnē'ha	(long house people), 7
Gat'go[n]'	(witchcraft), 27
Gawĕnnodŭs'hä	(compelling charm; charm used to compel persons to obey the charm holder), 29, 30
Gayänt'gogwus	(tobacco thrown down, " Dipped " Tobacco, a woman's name), 24
Go'diodia'se	(a lying tale, slander), 37
Gonoigä'nongi	(drunken), 20
Gowono[n]"gowa	(Large Talker, a name), 74
Gushĕdon'dada	(jug shaking dance), 101
Gwi"yă'	(an exclamation in the ganē'wo song), 85,

Hanĭssē'ono	(ha-nĭs-sē'-o-no, the devil), 18
Hadēiyäyo'	(new year announcers), 82
Hadidji'yontwŭs	(the new year ceremony), 75
Hadigoⁿ'săshoⁿo'	(False Face company), 127
Hadioⁿyä"geono	(they are messengers; the four angels), 19, 25
Hadiwĕnnoda'dies	(the thunderers), 98
Ha'dji'no	(male), 73
Haiyon'wĕntha	(Hai-yon'-wĕnt-ha, a sachemship title meaning, *he has lost it and searches, knowing where to find it*. The Seneca name for Hiawatha)
Hanä'sishĕ	(new year ceremonial officers), 82
Hasan'owānĕ'	(exalted name, the word applied to a chief), 44
Hătgwi'yot	(the son-in-law of Handsome Lake), 23
Hawĕni'o'	(good ruler, God; the name mostly used by the Christian Seneca), 48, 133
Hayänt'wŭtgŭs	(tobacco throwing ceremony), 121
Hĕnne'yoⁿ'	(a clairvoyant), 49
Hi"noⁿ	(the Thunderer), 104
Hodiänok'dooⁿ Hĕd'-iohe'	(the Creator), 19, 48
Honio"oⁿ	(white man), 20
Ho'noⁿ'gwae	(a nest), 47
Honon'diont	(overseer of the ceremonies), 411, 421
Hono"tcino"gä	(the guardian company), 116
Ho'tcine'gada	(company of charm holders; note that "tci" is pronounced as "*chee*" in *cheese*), 119
Hoyā'nĕ	(noble born, good in character, applied as a title to sachems. The Mohawk form Rhoya'nĕ' is sometimes translated "*lord*"), 9, 22
I"dos	(a charm society), 121, 122
Jodi"gwadoⁿ'	(a great horned serpent), 119
Joⁿgä'oⁿ	(elves of pygmies), 119
Joi'ise	(New Voice, a man's name), 76
Niagă'hos'sää'	(small bundle of magic substance), 29
Nia"gwahē	(great naked bear or mammoth bear, a mythical beast), 28; footnote, 40; 119

Nia'gwai"	(bear, bear ceremony), 125
Niawěⁿ'	(thanks are given), 36
Niawĕ"skänoⁿ'	(thank you, you are strong), a greeting, 133
Nïganĕga"a'	(little water) a medicine powder, 116
Niio'	(so be it, or it is well, "all right"), 22
Nis'a	(name of a month), 86
Nisko'wŭkni	(nĭs-ko'-wŭk-ni, the moon of midwinter), 6, 53
Notwai'shäⁿ	(spirit), 133
Oä'no'	(a dance, or society)
Odä'eo	(the veil over the world), 67
O'dän'kot	(Sunshine, a name), 117
Odjis'kwăthēⁿ	(Pudding Dry, a man's name), 24
O'g'i'wē	(the death chant, a ceremony), 21, 26, 50, 126
Ohī'ïo'	(river beautiful, name applied to the Allegany river), 20
Ondē'yä	(ceremonial officers, "buffalo robed"), 81
One'gă	(whiskey or rum), 9, 27
Oñgwe"oñwe	(real men, Iroquois), 18, 45
Oñgwe"oñwekä'	(Oñgwe"-oñwe-kä', literally, *men beings — real* — emphatically so), 6
Ono'ityi'yĕnde	(witch poison), 29, 72
Onondaga	(meaning, upon the hills)
Osto'wä'gō'wa	(Great Feather dance, the chief religious dance), 25, 42
Ot'go'ä	(wampum), 57
Otnä'yont	(sharp bone charm), 119
O'to'doⁿgwa"	(it is blazing, a ceremony), 123
Owa'ĕtgäⁿ	(road bad; a rough road), 69
O'wai'ta	(dried hand charm), 119
Sagoyĕ'wa'thă'	(pronounced Sa-go-yĕ'-wā-t'hă'; means, he keeps them awake. Name of Red Jacket, a Seneca leader and orator), 68
Sedékonĭ"	(you come to eat), 36
Sedē'tciä	(early in the morning), 6
Sedwä'gowä'nĕ'	(Se-dwä'-go-wä'-nĕ') Teacher-great, name applied to Handsome Lake, 71; footnote, 53; 67
Segaⁿ'hedŭs	(*He resurrects;* Christ), 67
Segoewa't'ha	(the tormentor, devil), 48

Segwai″doⁿgwi	(a man's name), 57
Sha″dotgéa	(the Eagle ceremony), 124
S'hagodiowěⁿ'gowa	(the false face spirit chief), 128
S'hondowěk'owa	(the death herald), 106
Skandyoⁿ″gwadĭ	(Seneca name of Owen Black Snake), 19
Skänoⁿ'	(strength, health), 133
Soi'kāgää″kwa	(night shining orb, the moon), 92
Sos'hēowă	(name of Handsome Lake's grandson and one of his successors, the grandfather of Gen. Ely S. Parker. English name was James Johnson), 12, 19
Soson'dowă	(S'o-son'-do-wă, *Night-Great,* the teacher of Handsome Lake's religious code. His English name is Edward Cornplanter, q. v.), 5, 16, 19, 80
Tää'wŏnyăs	(Awl Breaker, sometimes called Needle Breaker. The name of a Seneca chief), 23
Tă'dondä'ieha'	(a masculine proper name), 60
Tain'tciadě	(heaven world), 69
Tcäkowa	(pigeon dance), 82
Tci'gwagwa	(a ceremony), 123
Ti'sōt	(grandfather), 91
Waano″naogwā″ciot	(cornplanting ceremony), 101
Wa″da Tădinion'nio'o'	(maple thanksgiving), 102
Wadigusä'wea	(to throw up the paddle, meaning, "it is finished," a ceremonial term), 82
Wainonjää″koⁿ	(the death feast), 110
Wasa'z'ĕ	(Sioux; means also *warlike*), 103
Yai″kni	(month of May), 20
Yē'oⁿ'	(a woman), 33
Yeoⁿ'skwaswa'doⁿ'	(a thieving woman), 39
Ye'ondăthă	(the women s song ceremony), 21, 26
Yi'dōs	(a society having animal charms; the "Society of Mystic Animals": see I″dos), 121
Yotdondak'o'	(pygmy dance ceremony), 120
Yondwi'niasswā'yas	(she commits abortion), 30

INDEX

Abortion, 30; 30 (footnote)
Air regulator, 67
Allegany, 5, 6, 7, 15
Allegany Seneca, 15
Alphabet, 139
Anecdotes of Cornplanter, 136
Animal totem, 39; societies, 39; 40 (footnote), 113; ordered disbanded, 114; are ancient, 115; tabued, 115
Authorized teachers, 5
Avon, 9, 78

Bear, great naked, 119
Bear, mammoth, 28
Bear society, 125
Beauchamp, Dr William M., quoted, 127
Beaver, white, a charm, 119
Bible believers, 64
Blacksnake, Owen, 19
Blue panther, 119
Bluesky, William, 8
Boasting, denounced, 37
Buffalo Creek reservation treaty, 7, 64, 78
Buffaloes, sacred, 43
Buffalo society, 125; dance of, plate 17
Bundle, magic, 29

Cattaraugus, 5, 6
Cattaraugus, Seneca, 7, 15
Ceremony of herb gathering, 54
Ceremony, New Year (see Midwinter), 75
Ceremonies, special, 103
Charm, members, 119
Charms, witch, 28; Seneca name, 30; 30 (footnotes); corn, 54; society for, 119; good and evil, 120
Children, punishment of, 33; Handsome Lake's love of, 33 (footnote); treatment of, 34; warnings of, 34; sin of defaming, 35; hospitality toward, 36; destitute, 36
Christ, section 74, 67
Christian Indians, 6, 14
Christian influence, 11
Civil war, 13
Clairvoyant, 40
Cold Spring, 7, 12, 46, 76
Columbus, Christopher, 18
Command to preach, 26
Cooperation, 30
Conservative Indians, ideas, 14
Converts, 6, 7
Corn bug, 119
Cornplanter creek, 20
Cornplanter, Edward, photograph, plate 2, 5, 6, 8; quoted, 13; 132
Cornplanter (see also Gyantwaka or Gaiantwaka), 11
Cornplanter village, 12, 20, 61
Cornplanting thanksgiving, 54
Corn, spirit, 47; medicine, 54; planting of, 54; drawing, plate 12
Customs changed, 56
Customs, mourning, 107
Creator, 18, 19, 21, 22, 25, 26, 27 to 80; controversy with devil, 48

Dances, 30; four sanctioned, 41, 51, 124
Dark dance, 119
Daughter of Handsome Lake, 22
Dead man reviews, 24
Dearborn, General, letter from, 10
Death chant, 21, 126; drawing, plate 18
Death, coming of, a legend, 105
Death feast, 57, 126
Deer, sacred, 43
Devil, 101
Discovery of America, 16

Discussion between good and evil spirits, 48
Diviner, 49
Division of Iroquois, religious, 13, 55, 55 (footnote), 57
Dog, (*see* White dog), 66
Drunkenness, 9, 10, 20, 45, 54
Dry hand, 119

Eagle, society of, 124
Education, 38
Effects of Handsome Lake's religion, 10, 11; discussion of, 14
Effigies, 131
Elves, 119
Emotion, religious, 6
End of world, 44; signs of, 57; by fire, 59
Evil of drink, 54, 61
Evil spirit (*see also* Devil), 56, 59, 61

Fairies, 119
False Face company, 127; ceremony, 128
Family life, 32, 33; lack of children, 35; meals, 36; picture of, plate 4
Fees for healing, 56
Finger nail parings, 120
Five evils, the, 17, 18
Folk cults, 116; influence, 130
Four messengers, 24, 25, 77
Frauds against Iroquois, 10
Funeral customs, 57, 107; address, 107

Gaenendasaga, 12, 79
Gaiänt'wakă, 23, 50
Gai'wiio‘, 5; time of preaching, 6; present form, 7; as a divine message, 26
Ganeᵒⁿwoⁿ ceremony, 95
Ganio'dai'io (*see also* Handsome Lake), 9, 18, 19; teachings of, 20, 80, 114 (*see* glossary)
Gānoⁿ'wagĕs, 12, 78
Gardening, methods, 39 (footnote)
Gibson, Chief John, 6
Glossary of Seneca words
God (*see* Creator, Great Ruler, Good Minded)

Godiont, 41
Good Hunter, 117
Good Minded (*see* Good Spirit), 15, 31
Good Spirit (also Great Ruler and Good Minded), 15, 16, 19, 21, 105, 135
Grand River, 6, 131
Great Message, 27
Green corn ceremony, 43
Graves at Grand River, Ontario, plate 6

Handsome Lake, teachings of, 5; biography, 9; successful ministry, 10; value of his teaching, 11; revolutionized social life, 11; failures, 11; residence at Tonawanda, 11; ideas from Bible, 11; death, 13, 80; method of thinking, 21; sickness, 21; reviled, 47; influence of, 114
Handsome Lake's teachings, 27, 80, 114
Handsome Lake's monument, plate 9
Handsome Lake preaching, drawing, plate 15
Harrington, M. R., mentioned, 128
Harrison, Gen. William H., 66 (footnote)
Harvest song, 21
Heaven, *see* Three brothers, 134
Herald of death, 119
Herbs, medicine song of, 55; healing, 56
Honon'diont, 41, 42
Horned serpent, 119
House of Torment (also of punisher), 62; description, 63, 64, 70
Hunters, father and son, 52; murdered, 52
Huron, introduce the I"dos, 123
Hurricane, spirit, drawing, plate 19
Husk false faces, 129

Idea of soul, 61
I"dos ceremony, photograph of, plate 21
Indian religious communities, 7
Insanity, 47

Invocation over corn, 54
Iroquois Confederacy, 10
Iroquois disheartened, 10

Jacket, John, 7, 8
Jealousy, results of, 45 (footnote)
Jefferson, President Thomas, mentioned, 10
Journey over sky road, 62

Key to pronunciation, 130
Kittle, Chief Delos, quoted, 127

Lay, Skidmore, ceremony related by, 107
Life of Handsome Lake, 9
Life substance, 65
Little water company, 116
Logan, Chief Frank, 5
Long house, picture, plate 1; at Newtown, plate 3; at Tonawanda, plate 3; at Onondaga, plate 5; at Pine Woods, Cattaraugus, plate 5; Upper Cayuga, Grand River, Ont., plate 6; Seneca, Canada, plate 7; Onondaga, Canada, plate 8; environs of Cayuga, plate 8.

Magic animals, 119
Magic bundles, 29
Marriage, 31, 32
Masks, spirit, 123
Medicine outfit, picture, 118
Midwinter ceremony, 6; sanctioned, 51
Milky Way, 62 (footnote)
Moon dance, 103
Morgan, Lewis H., 12; quoted, 113
Morning song, 51
Mourning customs, 57, 107
Murderer discovered, drawing, plate 114

New religion, 5, 13, 115
Newtown, 7
New World, 47
Night song, 116

Obail, Henry, 11, 80 (footnote)
Old people, 35

Oneidas, Canadian, 8; mentioned, 14
Onĕg'ă (rum), 27
Onondaga, 7, 12, 14, 76, 78
Ostōwä'gō'wa, 42
Otters, society of, 121; drawing, plate 23

Parker, Gen. Ely S., 12; descendant of prophet, 12
Phonetic system, key to, 130
Pittsburgh, 20
Poison, secret, 20
Poverty, esteemed 15, 63 (footnote)
Progressive Indians, 14
Prophet, given power to see in earth, 49
Punishment for evil, 71, 72, 74
Purification, 77 (footnote)
Pygmy society, 119; opening ceremony, 120

Recitation, second day, 35; third day, 60
Red Jacket (see also Sagoyewatha) accused, 60 (footnote); punishment of, 68 (section 95)
Religion, Indian, 15
Repentance, song of, 29
Reservations, 5, 14
Revival, Indian religious, 6
Rites and ceremonies, notes on, 81
Road, narrow, 74
Road, sky, 62, 69, 70

St Regis, 7, 14
Secret medicine for corn, 54
Secret medicine societies, 113; tabued, 115
Seneca (see also Allegany, Cattaraugus and Tonawanda), 5
Serpent, 11; horned, 119
Sharp legs, 119
Sick man, drawing, plate 11
Sickness of Handsome Lake, 22
Sins, 44
Sisters of Diohe"ko", 126
Slander, 37
Societies, 40, 40 (footnote), 50, 113, 116, 130
Society of Friends, 10

Social relations of mankind, 36
Song, lost, 50
Sorrow, 57
Sos'hēowă, 12, 19
Soson'dowă (*see also* Edward Cornplanter), 16
Soul, ideas of, 61
Spirit of the corn, 47; drawing, plate 12
Stevens, Henry, 8
Stinginess, 62
Stone giant mask, 127
Strawberries, feast, 25; medicine, 25
Sun dance, 103
Sun myths, 131

Tää'wŏnyăs (Awl Breaker), 23
Thanksgiving, 51; song, 84
Three brothers, a legend, 132
Thunder dance, 103
Tobacco, 49
Tonawanda, 11, 12, 47, 68, 76
Tonawanda Seneca, 14
Tonwiisas, drawing of ceremony, plate 10
Tormentor, 48
Translation, 8
Trouble, time of, 20; drawing, plate 10
Tuscarora, 14

Unbelief in Gai'wiio', 57
Underworld, 43

Wampum, 6, 57
Warren, Pa., 20
War in heaven, 48
Warriors' charm, 30 (footnote)
Washington, George, 66, 137
White dog ceremony, 85; photograph, plate 20
White race, how it came to America, 16; Seneca name for, 3 (footnote), 20; economics of, 38
Whipping of foolish women, 46; drawing, plate 13
Wife, treatment of, 32
Wind spirit, 119; drawing, plate 19
Winter, ceremonies (*see* Midwinter)
Witchcraft, 27; 27–29 (footnote), 28
Witch doctors, 29 (footnote)
Women's dance, 21; drawing of, plate 16
Women's society, 126
Women's song, 21
Women, wise ways for, 37; foolish, whipped, 46
Wren, exploding, a charm, 119
Wright, Rev. Asher, 7; Mrs Wright, 135

New York State Education Department

New York State Museum

JOHN M. CLARKE, Director

PUBLICATIONS

Packages will be sent prepaid except when distance or weight renders the same impracticable. On 10 or more copies of any one publication 20% discount will be given. Editions printed are only large enough to meet special claims and probable sales. When the sale copies are exhausted, the price for the few reserve copies is advanced to that charged by second-hand booksellers, in order to limit their distribution to cases of special need. Such prices are inclosed in [ ]. All publications are in paper covers, unless binding is specified. Checks or money orders should be addressed and payable to New York State Education Department.

Museum annual reports 1847–date. *All in print to 1894, 50c a volume, 75c in cloth; 1894–date, sold in sets only; 75c each for octavo volumes; price of quarto volumes on application.*

These reports are made up of the reports of the Director, Geologist, Paleontologist, Botanist and Entomologist, and museum bulletins and memoirs, issued as advance sections of the reports.

Director's annual reports 1904–date.

1904.	138p. 20c.	1909.	230p. 41pl. 2 maps, 4 charts. *Out of print*
1905.	102p. 23pl. 30c.	1910.	280p. il. 42pl. 50
1906.	186p. 41pl. 25c.	1911.	218p. 49pl. 50c.
1907.	212p. 63pl. 50c.	1912.	*In press.*
1908.	234p. 39pl. map. 40c.		

These reports cover the reports of the State Geologist and of the State Paleontologist, bound also with the museum reports of which they form a part.

Geologist's annual reports 1881–date. Rep'ts 1, 3–13, 17–date, 8vo; 2, 14–16, 4to.

In 1898 the paleontologic work of the State was made distinct from the geologic and was reported separately from 1899–1903. The two departments were reunited in 1904, and are now reported in the Director's report.
The annual reports of the original Natural History Survey, 1837–41, are out of print.
Reports 1–4, 1881–84, were published only in separate form. Of the 5th report 4 pages were reprinted in the 39th museum report, and a supplement to the 6th report was included in the 40th museum report. The 7th and subsequent reports are included in the 41st and following museum reports, except that certain lithographic plates in the 11th report (1891) and 13th (1893) are omitted from the 45th and 47th museum reports.
Separate volumes of the following only are available.

Report	Price	Report	Price	Report	Price
12 (1892)	$.50	17	$.75	21	$.40
14	.75	18	.75	22	.40
15, 2v.	2	19	.40	23	.45
16	1	20	.50	[*See* Director's annual reports]	

Paleontologist's annual reports 1899–date.

See first note under Geologist's annual reports.
Bound also with museum reports of which they form a part. Reports for 1899 and 1900 may be had for 20c each. Those for 1901–3 were issued as bulletins. In 1904 combined with the Director's report.

Entomologist's annual reports on the injurious and other insects of the State of New York 1882–date.

Reports 3–20 bound also with museum reports 40–46, 48–58 of which they form a part. Since 1898 these reports have been issued as bulletins. Reports 3–4, 17 are out of print. Other reports with prices are:

NEW YORK STATE EDUCATION DEPARTMENT

Report	Price	Report	Price	Report	Price
1	$.50	11	$.25	21 (Bul. 104)	$.25
2	.30	12	.25	22 (" 110)	.25
5	.25	13	Out of print	23 (" 124)	.75
6	.15	14 (Bul. 23)	.20	24 (" 134)	.35
7	.20	15 (" 31)	.15	25 (" 141)	.35
8	.25	16 (" 36)	.25	26 (" 147)	.35
9	.25	18 (" 64)	.20	27 (" 155)	.40
10	.35	19 (" 67)	.15	28 *In press*	
		20 (" 97)	.40		

Reports 2, 8–12 may also be obtained bound in cloth at 25c each in addition to the price given above.

Botanist's annual reports 1867–date.

Bound also with museum reports 21–date of which they form a part; the first Botanist's report appeared in the 21st museum report and is numbered 21. Reports 21–24, 29, 31–41 were not published separately.

Separate reports for 1871–74, 1876, 1888–98 are out of print. Report for 1899 may be had for 20c; 1900 for 50c. Since 1901 these reports have been issued as bulletins.

Descriptions and illustrations of edible, poisonous and unwholesome fungi of New York have also been published in volumes 1 and 3 of the 48th (1894) museum report and in volume 1 of the 49th (1895), 51st (1897), 52d (1898), 54th (1900), 55th (1901), in volume 4 of the 56th (1902), in volume 2 of the 57th (1903), in volume 4 of the 58th (1904), in volume 2 of the 59th (1905), in volume 1 of the 60th (1906), in volume 2 of the 61st (1907), 62d (1908), 63d (1909), 64th (1910), 65th (1911) reports. The descriptions and illustrations of edible and unwholesome species contained in the 49th, 51st and 52d reports have been revised and rearranged, and, combined with others more recently prepared, constitute Museum Memoir 4.

Museum bulletins 1887–date. 8vo. *To advance subscribers, $2 a year, or $1 a year for division* (1) *geology, economic geology, paleontology, mineralogy;* 50c *each for division* (2) *general zoology, archeology, miscellaneous,* (3) *botany,* (4) *entomology.*

Bulletins are grouped in the list on the following pages according to divisions.
The divisions to which bulletins belong are as follows:

1 Zoology	55 Archeology	110 Entomology
2 Botany	56 Geology	111 Geology
3 Economic Geology	57 Entomology	112 Economic Geology
4 Mineralogy	58 Mineralogy	113 Archeology
5 Entomology	59 Entomology	114 Geology
6 "	60 Zoology	115 "
7 Economic Geology	61 Economic Geology	116 Botany
8 Botany	62 Miscellaneous	117 Archeology
9 Zoology	63 Geology	118 Geology
10 Economic Geology	64 Entomology	119 Economic Geology
11 "	65 Paleontology	120 "
12 "	66 Miscellaneous	121 Director's report for 1907
13 Entomology	67 Botany	122 Botany
14 Geology	68 Entomology	123 Economic Geology
15 Economic Geology	69 Paleontology	124 Entomology
16 Archeology	70 Mineralogy	125 Archeology
17 Economic Geology	71 Zoology	126 Geology
18 Archeology	72 Entomology	127 "
19 Geology	73 Archeology	128 "
20 Entomology	74 Entomology	129 Entomology
21 Geology	75 Botany	130 Zoology
22 Archeology	76 Entomology	131 Botany
23 Entomology	77 Geology	132 Economic Geology
24 "	78 Archeology	133 Director's report for 1908
25 Botany	79 Entomology	134 Entomology
26 Entomology	80 Paleontology	135 Geology
27 "	81 Geology	136 Entomology
28 Botany	82 "	137 Geology
29 Zoology	83 "	138 "
30 Economic Geology	84 "	139 Botany
31 Entomology	85 Economic Geology	140 Director's report for 1909
32 Archeology	86 Entomology	141 Entomology
33 Zoology	87 Archeology	142 Economic Geology
34 Geology	88 Zoology	143 "
35 Economic Geology	89 Archeology	144 Archeology
36 Entomology	90 Paleontology	145 Geology
37 "	91 Zoology	146 "
38 Zoology	92 Paleontology	147 Entomology
39 Paleontology	93 Economic Geology	148 Geology
40 Zoology	94 Botany	149 Director's report for 1910
41 Archeology	95 Geology	150 Botany
42 Geology	96 "	151 Economic Geology
43 Zoology	97 Entomology	152 Geology
44 Economic Geology	98 Mineralogy	153 "
45 Paleontology	99 Paleontology	154 "
46 Entomology	100 Economic Geology	155 Entomology
47 "	101 Paleontology	156 "
48 Geology	102 Economic Geology	157 Botany
49 Paleontology	103 Entomology	158 Director's report for 1911
50 Archeology	104 "	159 Geology
51 Zoology	105 Botany	160 "
52 Paleontology	106 Geology	161 Economic Geology
53 Entomology	107 Geology and Paleontology	162 Geology
54 Botany	108 Archeology	163 Archeology
	109 Entomology	

MUSEUM PUBLICATIONS

Bulletins are also found with the annual reports of the museum as follows:

ulletin	Report	Bulletin	Report	Bulletin	Report	Bulletin	Report
-15	48, v. 1	78	57, v. 2	116	60, v. 1	150	64, v. 2
, 17	50, v. 1	79	57, v. 1, pt 2	117	60, v. 3	151	64, v. 2
, 19	51, v. 1	80	57, v. 1, pt 1	118	60, v. 1	152	64, v. 2
-25	52, v. 1	81, 82	58, v. 3	119-21	61, v. 1	153	64, v. 2
-31	53, v. 1	83, 84	58, v. 1	122	61, v. 2	154	64, v. 2
-34	54, v. 1	85	58, v. 2	123	61, v. 2	155	65, v. 2
, 36	54, v. 2	86	58, v. 5	124	61, v. 2	156	65, v. 2
-44	54, v. 3	87-89	58, v. 4	125	62, v. 3	157	65, v. 2
-48	54, v. 4	90	58, v. 3	126-28	62, v. 1	158	65, v. 1
-54	55, v. 1	91	58, v. 4	129	62, v. 2	159	65, v. 1
	56, v. 4	92	58, v. 3	130	62, v. 3	160	65, v. 1
	56, v. 1	93	58, v. 2	131, 132	62, v. 1	161	65, v. 2
	56, v. 3	94	58, v. 4	133	62, v. 1	162	65, v. 1
	56, v. 1	95, 96	58, v. 1	134	62, v. 2		
, 60	56, v. 3	97	58, v. 5	135	63, v. 1	Memoir	
	56, v. 1	98, 99	59, v. 2	136	63, v. 2	2	49, v. 3
	56, v. 4	100	59, v. 1	137	63, v. 1	3, 4	53, v. 2
	56, v. 2	101	59, v. 2	138	63, v. 1	5, 6	57, v. 3
	56, v. 3	102	59, v. 1	139	63, v. 2	7	57, v. 4
	56, v. 2	103-5	59, v. 2	140	63, v. 1	8, pt 1	59, v. 3
, 67	56, v. 4	106	59, v. 1	141	63, v. 2	8, pt 2	59, v. 4
	56, v. 3	107	60, v. 2	142	63, v. 2	9, pt 1	60, v. 4
	56, v. 2	108	60, v. 3	143	63, v. 2	9, pt 2	62, v. 4
, 71	57, v. 1, pt 1	109, 110	60, v. 1	144	64, v. 2	10	60, v. 5
	57, v. 1, pt 2	111	60, v. 2	145	64, v. 1	11	61, v. 3
	57, v. 2	112	60, v. 1	146	64, v. 1	12	63, v. 3
	57, v. 1, pt 2	113	60, v. 3	147	64, v. 2	13	63, v. 4
	57, v. 2	114	60, v. 1	148	64, v. 1	14, v. 1	65, v. 3
	57, v. 1, pt 2	115	60, v. 2	149	64, v. 1	14, v. 2	65, v. 4
	57, v. 1, pt 1						

The figures at the beginning of each entry in the following list indicate its number as a useum bulletin.

eology and Paleontology. 14 Kemp, J. F. Geology of Moriah and Westport Townships, Essex Co. N. Y., with notes on the iron mines. 38p. il. 7pl. 2 maps. Sept. 1895. Free.

) Merrill, F. J. H. Guide to the Study of the Geological Collections of the New York State Museum. 164p. 119pl. map. Nov. 1898. *Out of print*.

: Kemp, J. F. Geology of the Lake Placid Region. 24p. 1pl. map. Sept. 1898. Free.

) Cumings, E. R. Lower Silurian System of Eastern Montgomery County; Prosser, C. S. Notes on the Stratigraphy of Mohawk Valley and Saratoga County, N. Y. 74p. 14pl. map. May 1900. 15c.

) Clarke, J. M.; Simpson, G. B. & Loomis, F. B. Paleontologic Papers 1. 72p. il. 16pl. Oct. 1900. 15c.

Contents: Clarke, J. M. A Remarkable Occurrence of Orthoceras in the Oneonta Beds of the Chenango Valley, N. Y.
—— Paropsonema cryptophya; a Peculiar Echinoderm from the Intumescens-zone (Portage Beds) of Western New York.
—— Dictyonine Hexactinellid Sponges from the Upper Devonic of New York.
—— The Water Biscuit of Squaw Island, Canandaigua Lake, N. Y.
Simpson, G. B. Preliminary Descriptions of New Genera of Paleozoic Rugose Corals.
Loomis, F. B. Siluric Fungi from Western New York.

: Ruedemann, Rudolf. Hudson River Beds near Albany and their Taxonomic Equivalents. 116p. 2pl. map. Apr. 1901. 25c.

; Grabau, A. W. Geology and Paleontology of Niagara Falls and Vicinity. 286p. il. 18pl. map. Apr. 1901. 65c; *cloth*, 90c.

) Woodworth, J. B. Pleistocene Geology of Nassau County and Borough of Queens. 58p. il. 8pl. map. Dec. 1901. 25c.

) Ruedemann, Rudolf; Clarke, J. M. & Wood, Elvira. Paleontologic Papers 2. 240p. 13pl. Dec. 1901. *Out of print*.

Contents: Ruedemann, Rudolf. Trenton Conglomerate of Rysedorph Hill.
Clarke, J. M. Limestones of Central and Western New York Interbedded with Bituminous Shales of the Marcellus Stage.
Wood, Elvira. Marcellus Limestones of Lancaster, Erie Co., N. Y.
Clarke, J. M. New Agelacrinites.
—— Value of Amnigenia as an Indicator of Fresh-water Deposits during the Devonic of New York, Ireland and the Rhineland.

: Clarke, J. M. Report of the State Paleontologist 1901. 280p. il. 10pl. map, 1 tab. July 1902. 40c.

) Merrill, F. J. H. Description of the State Geologic Map of 1901. 42p. 2 maps, tab. Nov. 1902. Free.

63 Clarke, J. M. & Luther, D. D. Stratigraphy of Canandaigua and Naples Quadrangles. 78p. map. June 1904. 25c.
65 Clarke, J. M. Catalogue of Type Specimens of Paleozoic Fossils in the New York State Museum. 848p. May 1903. $1.20, *cloth*.
69 —— Report of the State Paleontologist 1902. 464p. 52pl. 7 maps. Nov. 1903. $1. *cloth*.
77 Cushing, H. P. Geology of the Vicinity of Little Falls, Herkimer Co. 98p. il. 15pl. 2 maps. Jan. 1905. 30c.
80 Clarke, J. M. Report of the State Paleontologist 1903. 396p. 29pl. 2 maps Feb. 1905. 85c, *cloth*.
81 Clarke, J. M. & Luther, D. D. Watkins and Elmira Quadrangles. 32p. map. Mar. 1905. 25c.
82 —— Geologic Map of the Tully Quadrangle. 40p. map. Apr. 1905. 20c.
83 Woodworth, J. B. Pleistocene Geology of the Mooers Quadrangle. 62p. 25pl. map. June 1905. 25c.
84 —— Ancient Water Levels of the Champlain and Hudson Valleys. 206p. il. 11pl. 18 maps. July 1905. 45c.
90 Ruedemann, Rudolf. Cephalopoda of Beekmantown and Chazy Formations of Champlain Basin. 224p. il. 38pl. May 1906. 75c, *cloth*.
92 Grabau, A. W. Guide to the Geology and Paleontology of the Schoharie Region. 314p. il. 26pl. map. Apr. 1906. 75c, *cloth*.
95 Cushing, H. P. Geology of the Northern Adirondack Region. 188p. 15pl. 3 maps. Sept. 1905. 30c.
96 Ogilvie, I. H. Geology of the Paradox Lake Quadrangle. 54p. il. 17pl. map. Dec. 1905. 30c.
99 Luther, D. D. Geology of the Buffalo Quadrangle. 32p. map. May 1906. 20c.
101 —— Geology of the Penn Yan-Hammondsport Quadrangles. 28p. map. July 1906. *Out of print*.
106 Fairchild, H. L. Glacial Waters in the Erie Basin. 88p. 14pl 9 maps. Feb. 1907. *Out of print*.
107 Woodworth, J. B.; Hartnagel, C. A.; Whitlock, H. P.; Hudson, G. H.; Clarke, J. M.; White, David & Berkey, C. P. Geological Papers. 388p. 54pl. map. May 1907. 90c, *cloth*.
Contents: Woodworth, J. B. Postglacial Faults of Eastern New York.
Hartnagel, C. A. Stratigraphic Relations of the Oneida Conglomerate.
—— Upper Siluric and Lower Devonic Formations of the Skunnemunk Mountain Region.
Whitlock, H. P. Minerals from Lyon Mountain, Clinton Co.
Hudson, G. H. On Some Pelmatozoa from the Chazy Limestone of New York.
Clarke, J. M. Some New Devonic Fossils.
—— An Interesting Style of Sand-filled Vein.
—— Eurypterus Shales of the Shawangunk Mountains in Eastern New York.
White, David. A Remarkable Fossil Tree Trunk from the Middle Devonic of New York.
Berkey, C. P. Structural and Stratigraphic Features of the Basal Gneisses of the Highlands.
111 Fairchild, H. L. Drumlins of New York. 60p. 28pl. 19 maps. July 1907. *Out of print*.
114 Hartnagel, C. A. Geologic Map of the Rochester and Ontario Beach Quadrangles. 36p. map. Aug. 1907. 20c.
115 Cushing, H. P. Geology of the Long Lake Quadrangle. 88p. 20pl. map. Sept. 1907. *Out of print*.
118 Clarke, J. M. & Luther, D. D. Geologic Maps and Descriptions of the Portage and Nunda Quadrangles including a map of Letchworth Park. 50p. 16pl. 4 maps. Jan. 1908. 35c.
126 Miller, W. J. Geology of the Remsen Quadrangle. 54p. il. 11pl. map. Jan. 1909. 25c.
127 Fairchild, H. L. Glacial Waters in Central New York. 64p. 27pl. 15 maps. Mar. 1909. 40c.
128 Luther, D. D. Geology of the Geneva-Ovid Quadrangles. 44p. map. Apr. 1909. 20c.
135 Miller, W. J. Geology of the Port Leyden Quadrangle, Lewis County, N. Y. 62p. il. 11pl. map. Jan. 1910. 25c.
137 Luther, D. D. Geology of the Auburn-Genoa Quadrangles. 36p. map. Mar. 1910. 20c.
138 Kemp, J. F. & Ruedemann, Rudolf. Geology of the Elizabethtown and Port Henry Quadrangles. 176p. il. 20pl. 3 maps. Apr. 1910. 40c.

MUSEUM PUBLICATIONS

145 Cushing, H. P.; Fairchild, H. L.; Ruedemann, Rudolf & Smyth, C. H. Geology of the Thousand Islands Region. 194p. il. 62pl. 6 maps. Dec. 1910. 75c.
146 Berkey, C. P. Geologic Features and Problems of the New York City (Catskill) Aqueduct. 286p. il. 38pl. maps. Feb. 1911. 75c; *cloth*, $1.
148 Gordon, C. E. Geology of the Poughkeepsie Quadrangle. 122p. il. 26pl. map. Apr. 1911. 30c.
152 Luther, D. D. Geology of the Honeoye-Wayland Quadrangles. 30p. map. Oct. 1911. 20c.
153 Miller, William J. Geology of the Broadalbin Quadrangle, Fulton-Saratoga Counties, New York. 66p. il. 8 pl. map. Dec. 1911. 25c.
154 Stoller, James H. Glacial Geology of the Schenectady Quadrangle. 44p. 9 pl. map. Dec. 1911. 30c.
159 Kemp, James F. The Mineral Springs of Saratoga. 80p. il. 3pl. Apr. 1912. 15c.
160 Fairchild, H. L. Glacial Waters in the Black and Mohawk Valleys. 48p. il. 8pl. 14 maps. May 1912. 50c.
162 Ruedemann, Rudolf. The Lower Siluric Shales of the Mohawk Valley. 152p. il. 15pl. Aug. 1912. 35c.
Miller, William J. Geological History of New York State. *In press.*
Luther, D. D. Geology of the Attica and Depew Quadrangles. *In press.*
Miller, William J. Geology of the North Creek Quadrangle. *In press.*
Luther, D. D. Geology of the Phelps Quadrangle. *In preparation.*
Whitnall, H. O. Geology of the Morrisville Quadrangle. *Prepared.*
Hopkins, T. C. Geology of the Syracuse Quadrangle. *Prepared.*
Hudson, G. H. Geology of Valcour Island. *In preparation.*

Economic Geology. 3 Smock, J. C. Building Stone in the State of New York. 154p. Mar. 1888. *Out of print.*
7 — — First Report on the Iron Mines and Iron Ore Districts in the State of New York. 78p. map. June 1889. *Out of print.*
10 — — Building Stone in New York. 210p. map. tab. Sept. 1890. 40c.
11 Merrill, F. J. H. Salt and Gypsum Industries of New York. 94p. 12pl. 2 maps, 11 tab. Apr. 1893. [50c]
12 Ries, Heinrich. Clay Industries of New York. 174p. il. 1pl. map. Mar. 1895. 30c.
15 Merrill, F. J. H. Mineral Resources of New York. 240p. 2 maps. Sept. 1895. [50c]
17 — — Road Materials and Road Building in New York. 52p. 14 pl. 2 maps. Oct. 1897. 15c.
30 Orton, Edward. Petroleum and Natural Gas in New York. 136p. il. 3 maps. Nov. 1899. 15c.
35 Ries, Heinrich. Clays of New York; their Properties and Uses. 450p. 140pl. map. June 1900. *Out of print.*
44 — — Lime and Cement Industries of New York; Eckel, E. C. Chapters on the Cement Industry. 332p. 101pl. 2 maps. Dec. 1901. 85c; *cloth*.
61 Dickinson, H. T. Quarries of Bluestone and Other Sandstones in New York. 114p. 18pl. 2 maps. Mar. 1903. 35c.
85 Rafter, G. W. Hydrology of New York State. 902p. il. 44pl. 5 maps. May 1905. $1.50, *cloth*.
93 Newland, D. H. Mining and Quarry Industry of New York. 78p. July 1905. *Out of print.*
100 McCourt, W. E. Fire Tests of Some New York Building Stones. 40p. 26pl. Feb. 1906. 15c.
102 Newland, D. H. Mining and Quarry Industry of New York 1905. 162p. June 1906. 25c.
112 — — Mining and Quarry Industry of New York 1906. 82p. July 1907. *Out of print.*
119 — — & Kemp, J. F. Geology of the Adirondack Magnetic Iron Ores with a Report on the Mineville-Port Henry Mine Group. 184p. 14pl. 8 maps. Apr. 1908. 35c.
120 Newland, D. H. Mining and Quarry Industry of New York 1907. 82p. July 1908. *Out of print.*
123 — — & Hartnagel, C. A. Iron Ores of the Clinton Formation in New York State. 76p. il. 14pl. 3 maps. Nov. 1908. 25c.
132 Newland, D. H. Mining and Quarry Industry of New York 1908. 98p. July 1909. 15c.

142 —— Mining and Quarry Industry of New York for 1909. 98p. Aug. 1910. 15c.
143 —— Gypsum Deposits of New York. 94p. 20pl. 4 maps. Oct. 1910. 35c.
151 —— Mining and Quarry Industry of New York 1910. 82p. June 1911. 15c.
161 —— Mining and Quarry Industry of New York 1911. 114p. July 1912. 20c.
Mineralogy. 4 Nason, F. L. Some New York Minerals and their Localities. 22p. 1pl. Aug. 1888. *Free.*
58 Whitlock, H. P. Guide to the Mineralogic Collections of the New York State Museum. 150p. il. 39pl. 11 models. Sept. 1902. 40c.
70 —— New York Mineral Localities. 110p. Oct. 1903. 20c.
98 —— Contributions from the Mineralogic Laboratory. 38p. 7pl. Dec. 1905. *Out of print.*
Zoology. 1 Marshall, W. B. Preliminary List of New York Unionidae. 20p. Mar. 1892. *Free.*
9 —— Beaks of Unionidae Inhabiting the Vicinity of Albany, N. Y. 30p. 1pl. Aug. 1890. *Free.*
29 Miller, G. S., jr. Preliminary List of New York Mammals. 124p. Oct. 1899. 15c.
33 Farr, M. S. Check List of New York Birds. 224p. Apr. 1900. 25c.
38 Miller, G. S., jr. Key to the Land Mammals of Northeastern North America. 106p. Oct. 1900. *Out of print.*
40 Simpson, G. B. Anatomy and Physiology of Polygyra albolabris and Limax maximus and Embryology of Limax maximus. 82p. 28pl. Oct. 1901. 25c.
43 Kellogg, J. L. Clam and Scallop Industries of New York. 36p. 2pl. map. Apr. 1901. *Free.*
51 Eckel, E. C. & Paulmier, F. C. Catalogue of Reptiles and Batrachians of New York. 64p. il. 1pl. Apr. 1902. *Out of print.*
Eckel, E. C. Serpents of Northeastern United States.
Paulmier, F. C. Lizards, Tortoises and Batrachians of New York.
60 Bean, T. H. Catalogue of the Fishes of New York. 784p. Feb. 1903. $1, *cloth.*
71 Kellogg, J. L. Feeding Habits and Growth of Venus mercenaria. 30p. 4pl. Sept. 1903. *Free.*
88 Letson, Elizabeth J. Check List of the Mollusca of New York. 116p. May 1905. 20c.
91 Paulmier, F. C. Higher Crustacea of New York City. 78p. il. June 1905. 20c.
130 Shufeldt, R. W. Osteology of Birds. 382p. il. 26pl. May 1909. 50c.
Entomology. 5 Lintner, J. A. White Grub of the May Beetle. 34p. il. Nov. 1888. *Free.*
6 —— Cut-worms. 38p. il. Nov. 1888. *Free.*
13 —— San José Scale and Some Destructive Insects of New York State. 54p. 7pl. Apr. 1895. 15c.
20 Felt, E. P. Elm Leaf Beetle in New York State. 46p. il. 5pl. June 1898. *Free.*
See 57.

23 —— 14th Report of the State Entomologist 1898. 150p. il. 9pl. Dec. 1898. 20c.
24 —— Memorial of the Life and Entomologic Work of J. A. Lintner Ph.D. State Entomologist 1874–98; Index to Entomologist's Reports 1–13. 316p. 1pl. Oct. 1899. 35c.
Supplement to 14th report of the State Entomologist.

26 —— Collection, Preservation and Distribution of New York Insects 36p. il. Apr. 1899. *Free.*
27 —— Shade Tree Pests in New York State. 26p. il. 5pl. May 1899. *Free.*
31 —— 15th Report of the State Entomologist 1899. 128p. June 1900. 15c.
36 —— 16th Report of the State Entomologist 1900. 118p. 16pl. Mar. 1901. 25c.
37 —— Catalogue of Some of the More Important Injurious and Beneficial Insects of New York State. 54p. il. Sept. 1900. *Free.*

—— Scale Insects of Importance and a List of the Species in New York State. 94p. il. 15pl. June 1901. 25c.

Needham, J. G. & Betten, Cornelius. Aquatic Insects in the Adirondacks. 234p. il. 36pl. Sept. 1901. 45c.

Felt, E. P. 17th Report of the State Entomologist 1901. 232p. il. 6pl. Aug. 1902. *Out of print.*

—— Elm Leaf Beetle in New York State. 46p. il. 8pl. Aug. 1902. *Out of print.*

This is a revision of Bulletin 20 containing the more essential facts observed since that is prepared.

—— Grapevine Root Worm. 40p. 6pl. Dec. 1902. 15c.

See 72.

—— 18th Report of the State Entomologist 1902. 110p. 6pl. May 1903. 20c.

Needham, J. G. *& others.* Aquatic Insects in New York. 322p. 52pl. Aug. 1903. 80c, *cloth.*

Felt, E. P. Grapevine Root Worm. 58p. 13pl. Nov. 1903. 20c.

This is a revision of Bulletin 59 containing the more essential facts observed since that is prepared.

—— & Joutel, L. H. Monograph of the Genus Saperda. 88p. 14pl. June 1904. 25c.

Felt, E. P. 19th Report of the State Entomologist 1903. 150p. 4pl. 1904. 15c.

—— Mosquitos or Culicidae of New York. 164p. il. 57pl. tab. Oct. 1904. 40c.

Needham, J. G. *& others.* May Flies and Midges of New York. 352p. il. 37pl. June 1905. 80c, *cloth.*

Felt, E. P. 20th Report of the State Entomologist 1904. 246p. il. 19pl. Nov. 1905. 40c.

—— Gipsy and Brown Tail Moths. 44p. 10pl. July 1906. 15c.

—— 21st Report of the State Entomologist 1905. 144p. 10pl. Aug. 1906. 25c.

—— Tussock Moth and Elm Leaf Beetle. 34p. 8pl. Mar. 1907. 20c.

—— 22d Report of the State Entomologist 1906. 152p. 3pl. June 1907. 25c.

—— 23d Report of the State Entomologist 1907. 542p. il. 44pl. Oct. 1908. 75c.

—— Control of Household Insects. 48p. il. May 1909. *Out of print.*

—— 24th Report of the State Entomologist 1908. 208p. il. 17pl. Sept. 1909. 35c.

—— Control of Flies and Other Household Insects. 56p. il. Feb. 1910. 15c.

This is a revision of Bulletin 129 containing the more essential facts observed since at was prepared.

Felt, E. P. 25th Report of the State Entomologist 1909. 178p. il. 22pl. July 1910. 35c.

—— 26th Report of the State Entomologist 1910. 182p. il. 35pl. Mar. 1911. 35c.

—— 27th Report of the State Entomologist 1911. 198p. il. 27pl. Jan. 1912. 40c.

—— Elm Leaf Beetle and White-Marked Tussock Moth. 35p. 8pl. Jan. 1912. 20c.

—— 28th Report of the State Entomologist 1912. *In press.*

Needham, J. G. Monograph on Stone Flies. *In preparation.*

Botany. 2 Peck, C. H. Contributions to the Botany of the State of New York. 72p. 2pl. May 1887. *Out of print.*

—— Boleti of the United States. 98p. Sept. 1889. *Out of print.*

—— Report of the State Botanist 1898. 76p. 5pl. Oct. 1899. *Out of print.*

—— Plants of North Elba. 206p. map. June 1899. 20c.

—— Report of the State Botanist 1901. 58p. 7pl. Nov. 1902. 40c.

—— Report of the State Botanist 1902. 196p. 5pl. May 1903. 50c.

—— Report of the State Botanist 1903. 70p. 4pl. 1904. 40c.

—— Report of the State Botanist 1904. 60p. 10pl. July 1905. 40c.

105 —— Report of the State Botanist 1905. 108p. 12pl. Aug. 1906. 50c.
116 —— Report of the State Botanist 1906. 120p. 6pl. July 1907. 35c.
122 —— Report of the State Botanist 1907. 178p. 5pl. Aug. 1908. 40c.
131 —— Report of the State Botanist 1908. 202p. 4pl. July 1909. 40c.
139 —— Report of the State Botanist 1909. 116p. 10pl. May 1910. 45c.
150 —— Report of the State Botanist 1910. 100p. 5pl. May 1911. 30c.
157 —— Report of the State Botanist 1911. 139p. 9pl. Mar. 1912. 35c.
—— Report of the State Botanist 1912. *In press.*

Archeology. 16 Beauchamp, W. M. Aboriginal Chipped Stone Implements of New York. 86p. 23pl. Oct. 1897. 25c.
18 —— Polished Stone Articles Used by the New York Aborigines. 104p. 35pl. Nov. 1897. 25c.
22 —— Earthenware of the New York Aborigines. 78p. 33pl. Oct. 1898. 25c.
32 —— Aboriginal Occupation of New York. 190p. 16pl. 2 maps. Mar. 1900. 30c.
41 —— Wampum and Shell Articles Used by New York Indians. 166p. 28pl. Mar. 1901. 30c.
50 —— Horn and Bone Implements of the New York Indians. 112p. 43pl. Mar. 1902. 30c.
55 —— Metallic Implements of the New York Indians. 94p. 38pl. June 1902. 25c.
73 —— Metallic Ornaments of the New York Indians. 122p. 37pl. Dec. 1903. 30c.
78 —— History of the New York Iroquois. 340p. 17pl. map. Feb. 1905. 75c, *cloth.*
87 —— Perch Lake Mounds. 84p. 12pl. Apr. 1905. *Out of print.*
89 —— Aboriginal Use of Wood in New York. 190p. 35pl. June 1905. 35c.
108 —— Aboriginal Place Names of New York. 336p. May 1907. 40c.
113 —— Civil, Religious and Mourning Councils and Ceremonies of Adoption. 118p. 7pl. June 1907. 25c.
117 Parker, A. C. An Erie Indian Village and Burial Site. 102p. 38pl. Dec. 1907. 30c.
125 Converse, H. M. & Parker, A. C. Iroquois Myths and Legends. 196p. il. 11pl. Dec. 1908. 50c.
144 Parker, A. C. Iroquois Uses of Maize and Other Food Plants. 120p. il. 31pl. Nov. 1910. 30c.
163 Parker, A. C. The Code of Handsome Lake. 144p. 23pl. Nov. 1912. 25c.

Miscellaneous. 62 Merrill, F. J. H. Directory of Natural History Museums in United States and Canada. 236p. Apr. 1903. 30c.
66 Ellis, Mary. Index to Publications of the New York State Natural History Survey and New York State Museum 1837–1902. 418p. June 1903. 75c, *cloth.*

Museum memoirs 1889–date. 4to.
1 Beecher, C. E. & Clarke, J. M. Development of Some Silurian Brachiopoda. 96p. 8pl. Oct. 1889. $1.
2 Hall, James & Clarke, J. M. Paleozoic Reticulate Sponges. 350p. il. 70pl. 1898. $2, *cloth.*
3 Clarke, J. M. The Oriskany Fauna of Becraft Mountain, Columbia Co., N. Y. 128p. 9pl. Oct. 1900. 80c.
4 Peck, C. H. N. Y. Edible Fungi, 1895–99. 106p. 25pl. Nov. 1900. [$1.25]

This includes revised descriptions and illustrations of fungi reported in the 49th, 51st and 52d reports of the State Botanist.

5 Clarke, J. M. & Ruedemann, Rudolf. Guelph Formation and Fauna of New York State. 196p. 21pl. July 1903. $1.50, *cloth.*
6 Clarke, J. M. Naples Fauna in Western New York. 268p. 26pl. map. 1904. $2, *cloth.*
7 Ruedemann, Rudolf. Graptolites of New York. Pt 1 Graptolites of the Lower Beds. 350p. 17pl. Feb. 1905. $1.50, *cloth.*
8 Felt, E. P. Insects Affecting Park and Woodland Trees. v.1. 460p. il. 48pl. Feb. 1906. $2.50, *cloth*; v. 2. 548p. il. 22pl. Feb. 1907. $2, *cloth.*
9 Clarke, J. M. Early Devonic of New York and Eastern North America. Pt 1. 366p. il. 70pl. 5 maps. Mar. 1908. $2.50, *cloth*; Pt 2. 250p. il. 36pl. 4 maps. Sept. 1909. $2, *cloth.*

MUSEUM PUBLICATIONS

10 Eastman, C. R. The Devonic Fishes of the New York Formations. 236p. 15pl. 1907. $1.25, *cloth*.
11 Ruedemann, Rudolf. Graptolites of New York. Pt 2 Graptolites of the Higher Beds. 584p. il. 31pl. 2 tab. Apr. 1908. $2.50, *cloth*.
12 Eaton, E. H. Birds of New York. v. 1. 501p. il. 42pl. Apr. 1910. $3, *cloth*; v. 2, *in press*.
13 Whitlock, H. P. Calcites of New York. 190p. il. 27pl. Oct. 1910. $1, *cloth*.
14 Clarke, J. M. & Ruedemann, Rudolf. The Eurypterida of New York. v. 1. Text. 440p. il. v. 2 Plates. 188p. 88pl. Dec. 1912. $4, *cloth*.

Natural History of New York. 30v. il. pl. maps. 4to. Albany 1842–94.

DIVISION 1 ZOOLOGY. De Kay, James E. Zoology of New York; or, The New York Fauna; comprising detailed descriptions of all the animals hitherto observed within the State of New York with brief notices of those occasionally found near its borders, and accompanied by appropriate illustrations. 5v. il. pl. maps. sq. 4to. Albany 1842–44. *Out of print*.

Historical introduction to the series by Gov. W. H. Seward. 178p.

v. 1 pt 1 Mammalia. 131 + 46p. 33pl. 1842.
  300 copies with hand-colored plates.

v. 2 pt 2 Birds. 12 + 380p. 141pl. 1844.
  Colored plates.

v. 3 pt 3 Reptiles and Amphibia. 7 + 98p. pt 4 Fishes. 15 + 415p. 1842.
  pt 3–4 bound together.

v. 4 Plates to accompany v. 3. Reptiles and Amphibia. 23pl. Fishes. 79pl. 1842.
  300 copies with hand-colored plates.

v. 5 pt 5 Mollusca. 4 + 271p. 40pl. pt 6 Crustacea. 70p. 13pl. 1843–44.
  Hand-colored plates; pts 5–6 bound together.

DIVISION 2 BOTANY. Torrey, John. Flora of the State of New York; comprising full descriptions of all the indigenous and naturalized plants hitherto discovered in the State, with remarks on their economical and medical properties. 2v. il. pl. sq. 4to. Albany 1843. *Out of print*.

v. 1 Flora of the State of New York. 12 + 484p. 72pl. 1843.
  300 copies with hand-colored plates.

v. 2 Flora of the State of New York. 572p. 89pl. 1843.
  300 copies with hand-colored plates.

DIVISION 3 MINERALOGY. Beck, Lewis C. Mineralogy of New York; comprising detailed descriptions of the minerals hitherto found in the State of New York, and notices of their uses in the arts and agriculture. il. pl. sq. 4to. Albany 1842. *Out of print*.

v. 1 pt 1 Economical Mineralogy. pt 2 Descriptive Mineralogy. 24 + 536p. 1842.
  8 plates additional to those printed as part of the text.

DIVISION 4 GEOLOGY. Mather, W. W.; Emmons, Ebenezer; Vanuxem, Lardner & Hall, James. Geology of New York. 4v. il. pl. sq. 4to. Albany 1842–43. *Out of print*.

v. 1 pt 1 Mather, W. W. First Geological District. 37 + 653p. 46pl. 1843.
v. 2 pt 2 Emmons, Ebenezer. Second Geological District. 10 + 437p. 17pl. 1842.
v. 3 pt 3 Vanuxem, Lardner. Third Geological District. 306p. 1842.
v. 4 pt 4 Hall, James. Fourth Geological District. 22 + 683p. 19pl. map. 1843.

DIVISION 5 AGRICULTURE. Emmons, Ebenezer. Agriculture of New York; comprising an account of the classification, composition and distribution of the soils and rocks and the natural waters of the different geological formations, together with a condensed view of the meteorology and agricultural productions of the State. 5v. il. pl. sq. 4to. Albany 1846–54. *Out of print*.

v. 1 Soils of the State, their Composition and Distribution. 11 + 371p. 21pl. 1846.
v. 2 Analysis of Soils, Plants, Cereals, etc. 8 + 343 + 46p. 42pl. 1849.
   With hand-colored plates.
v. 3 Fruits, etc. 8 + 340p. 1851.
v. 4 Plates to accompany v. 3. 95pl. 1851.
   Hand-colored.
v. 5 Insects Injurious to Agriculture. 8 + 272p. 50pl. 1854.
   With hand-colored plates.

DIVISION 6 PALEONTOLOGY. Hall, James. Palaeontology of New York. 8v. il. pl. sq. 4to. Albany 1847-94. *Bound in cloth.*
v. 1 Organic Remains of the Lower Division of the New York System. 23 + 338p. 99pl. 1847. *Out of print.*
v. 2 Organic Remains of Lower Middle Division of the New York System. 8 + 362p. 104pl. 1852. *Out of print.*
v. 3 Organic Remains of the Lower Helderberg Group and the Oriskany Sandstone. pt 1, text. 12 + 532p. 1859. [$3.50]
—— pt 2. 142pl. 1861. [$2.50]
v. 4 Fossil Brachiopoda of the Upper Helderberg, Hamilton, Portage and Chemung Groups. 11 + 1 + 428p. 69pl. 1867. $2.50.
v. 5 pt 1 Lamellibranchiata 1. Monomyaria of the Upper Helderbergs, Hamilton and Chemung Groups. 18 + 268p. 45pl. 1884. $2.50.
—— —— Lamellibranchiata 2. Dimyaria of the Upper Helderberg, Hamilton, Portage and Chemung Groups. 62 + 293p. 51pl. 1885. $2.50.
—— pt 2 Gasteropoda, Pteropoda and Cephalopoda of the Upper Helderberg, Hamilton, Portage and Chemung Groups. 2v. 1879. v. 1, text. 15 + 492p.; v.2. 120pl. $2.50 for 2 v.
—— & Simpson, George B. v. 6 Corals and Bryozoa of the Lower and Upper Helderberg and Hamilton Groups. 24 + 298p. 67pl. 1887. $2.50.
—— & Clarke, John M. v. 7 Trilobites and Other Crustacea of the Oriskany, Upper Helderberg, Hamilton, Portage, Chemung and Catskill Groups. 64 + 236p. 46pl. 1888. Cont. supplement to v. 5, pt 2. Pteropoda, Cephalopoda and Annelida. 42p. 18pl. 1888. $2.50.
—— & Clarke, John M. v. 8 pt 1 Introduction to the Study of the Genera of the Paleozoic Brachiopoda. 16 + 367p. 44pl. 1892. $2.50.
—— & Clarke, John M. v. 8 pt 2 Paleozoic Brachiopoda. 16 + 394p. 64pl. 1894. $2.50.

Catalogue of the Cabinet of Natural History of the State of New York and of the Historical and Antiquarian Collection annexed thereto. 242p. 8vo. 1853.

Handbooks 1893–date.

New York State Museum. 52p. il. 1902. Free.
   Outlines, history and work of the museum with list of staff 1902.

Paleontology. 12p. 1899. *Out of print.*
   Brief outline of State Museum work in paleontology under heads: Definition; Relation to biology; Relation to stratigraphy; History of paleontology in New York.

Guide to Excursions in the Fossiliferous Rocks of New York. 124p. 1899. Free.
   Itineraries of 32 trips covering nearly the entire series of Paleozoic rocks, prepared specially for the use of teachers and students desiring to acquaint themselves more intimately with the classic rocks of this State.

Entomology. 16p. 1899. *Out of print.*
Economic Geology. 44p. 1904. Free.
Insecticides and Fungicides. 20p. 1909. Free.
Classification of New York Series of Geologic Formations. 32p. 1903. *Out of print.* Revised edition. 96p. 1912. Free.

Geologic maps. Merrill, F. J. H. Economic and Geologic Map of the State of New York; issued as part of Museum Bulletin 15 and 48th Museum Report, v. 1. 59 x 67 cm. 1894. Scale 14 miles to 1 inch. 15c.

—— Map of the State of New York Showing the Location of Quarries of Stone Used for Building and Road Metal. 1897. *Out of print.*

—— Map of the State of New York Showing the Distribution of the Rocks Most Useful for Road Metal. 1897. *Out of print.*

—— Geologic Map of New York. 1901. Scale 5 miles to 1 inch. *In atlas form $3. Lower Hudson sheet* 60c.

The lower Hudson sheet, geologically colored, covers Rockland, Orange, Dutchess, Putnam, Westchester, New York, Richmond, Kings, Queens and Nassau counties, and parts of Sullivan, Ulster and Suffolk counties; also northeastern New Jersey and part of western Connecticut.

—— Map of New York Showing the Surface Configuration and Water Sheds. 1901. Scale 12 miles to 1 inch. 15c.

—— Map of the State of New York Showing the Location of its Economic Deposits. 1904. Scale 12 miles to 1 inch. 15c.

Geologic maps on the United States Geological Survey topographic base. Scale 1 in. = 1 m. Those marked with an asterisk have also been published separately.

*Albany county. 1898. *Out of print.*
Area around Lake Placid. 1898.
Vicinity of Frankfort Hill [parts of Herkimer and Oneida counties]. 1899.
Rockland county. 1899.
Amsterdam quadrangle. 1900.
*Parts of Albany and Rensselaer counties. 1901.
*Niagara river. 1901. 25c.
Part of Clinton county. 1901.
Oyster Bay and Hempstead quadrangles on Long Island. 1901.
Portions of Clinton and Essex counties. 1902.
Part of town of Northumberland, Saratoga co. 1903.
Union Springs, Cayuga county and vicinity. 1903.
*Olean quadrangle. 1903. Free.
*Becraft Mt with 2 sheets of sections. (Scale 1 in. = 1 m.) 1903. 20c.
*Canandaigua-Naples quadrangles. 1904. 20c.
*Little Falls quadrangle. 1905. Free.
*Watkins-Elmira quadrangles. 1905. 20c.
*Tully quadrangle. 1905. Free.
*Salamanca quadrangle. 1905. Free.
*Mooers quadrangle. 1905. Free.
Paradox Lake quadrangle. 1905.
*Buffalo quadrangle. 1906. Free.
*Penn Yan-Hammondsport quadrangles. 1906. 20c.
*Rochester and Ontario Beach quadrangles. 20c.
*Long Lake quadrangle. Free.
*Nunda-Portage quadrangles. 20c.
*Remsen quadrangle. 1908. Free.
*Geneva-Ovid quadrangles. 1909. 20c.
*Port Leyden quadrangle. 1910. Free.
*Auburn-Genoa quadrangles. 1910. 20c.
*Elizabethtown and Port Henry quadrangles. 1910. 15c.
*Alexandria Bay quadrangle. Free.
*Cape Vincent quadrangle. Free.
*Clayton quadrangle. Free.
*Grindstone quadrangle. Free.
*Theresa quadrangle. Free.
*Poughkeepsie quadrangle. Free.
*Honeoye-Wayland quadrangle. 20c.
*Broadalbin quadrangle. Free.
*Schenectady quadrangle. Free.

Dylan - Unplugge
John Lee Hooker - The Healer
  "   "   "   - Best Of Friends
Howlin Wolf - Box-set
Muddy Waters - "   "

info@ebweb.ca